Testimonials:

"Embarking on the journey of 'Swipe for Mr. Right' revealed a refreshing perspective on timeless wisdom. It was an insightful book that resonated deeply, reminding me that love begins with self-love, rooted in self awareness. This book, a beacon of hope for those searching for authentic connections will give you the practical guide you need to uphold your standards and help you value your unique and irreplaceable worth as a woman.

I am Grateful for this transformative guide and the wisdom it imparts. I Highly recommended it for everyone seeking true and authentic love."

- January Donovan
Founder, The Wholeness School & The Woman School

Brilliant! The author walks her talk. Too many books talk about the subject of love from an academic position. Finally, here's an author who has gone through heartbreak only to learn from it and put it into a step-by-step guide to finding love success.

- Eric Lofholm,
President of Eric Lofholm International, Author of Continuous Sales Improvement, The System & many other sales books...

"Dr. Renée's brilliance as a Love & Relationship coach is unparalleled. 'Swipe for Mr. Right' isn't just a book; it's a roadmap to lasting love. Married happily for over 20 years, her insights have fortified our bond, making every day a celebration of enduring love. Grateful for her wisdom."

- Steve & Jennie Erickson
EventRaptor Marketing Team

"Every now and then a book comes along that provides the right perspective at the right time. Swipe for Mr. Right is one of those books. You can't build solid life together as a couple without loving yourself first. I know this because I have been married for over 21 wonderful years to my beloved, Bruce. Dr. Renée has done an amazing job in helping couples grow and flourish!"

- Deb Ellis
Financial Advisor, Author of Your Money & You and Women & Wealth

"Enormous gratitude to my exceptional love and relationship coach, the mastermind behind 'Swipe for Mr. Right.' Her insights and strategies not only guided my journey to love but also paved the way for 19 blissful years with my wife. As a financial planner, her wisdom transcends professional and personal realms. Forever thankful for the fulfilling relationship she helped me build. Thank you!"

- Gary Handler
Financial Planner, & Gary's "Queen" Cathleen

It's a rarity to find an author that sees the full perspective of attracting your perfect mate and explain it in simple terms. Powerful stories inspire you to see where you need to take your love life to the next level and catapult your new relationship to the next level. A real game changer!

- Napoleon Gratitude
Founder & CEO of Givit and Creator & Founder of M8CALL Events

Dr. Love's Swipe for Mr. Right is a masterpiece that transcends the realm of relationships. As a financial & retirement advisor, navigating the complexities of love wasn't my expertise, but Dr. Renée's book became my guiding light. It's more than a book; it's a love mentor that brought profound impact to my relationship journey. The pearls of wisdom embedded in Swipe for Mr. Right transformed my outlook on love, helping me navigate the intricacies with newfound clarity. I am truly grateful for the soulful connection it led me to. Dr. Renée's insights resonate beyond matters of the heart, touching every facet of life. Her book is a beacon of wisdom, offering valuable lessons that extend far beyond the pages, enriching not just our relationships but our entire existence.

- Milan Schwarzkopf
 # 1 Purposeful Retirement Expert, teaching how to best arrange and live through retirement. Author of Living Your Best Third Act; How to Be Healthy, Wealthy, and Happy in your Retirement

"Bravo to my incredible love and relationship coach for the masterpiece, 'Swipe for Mr. Right.' This book is a treasure trove of wisdom, unraveling the secrets to navigating online love with grace and authenticity. It's more than a guide; it's a transformative journey to self-discovery and attracting the love we deserve. A must-read for anyone seeking genuine connections in the digital age!"

- Nicole Grey
Real Estate Expert and Author of Who's the Baby? Who's the Boyfriend?

"Dr. Renée Michelle Gordon is one of those rare individual who is the real deal. She is brilliant when it comes to showing you how to inspire couples on a daily basis and get the best out of them. Do yourself a favor and read Dr. Renée's book, get her coaching and apply her message to your life so you can soar!"

- Diana Zwein
Financial Professional, Author of The Long Goodbye

"Single available people have been waiting for a book like this to come along for a long time. Dr. Renée understands the power of building a strong connection by first loving yourself. I've been happily married for over 25 blissful years. Buy this book and attract your ideal life partner!"

- Mary West
Founder of "The Mary West Network" & Producer of The Patrick and Mary Unstoppable Author Interview Series

"Dr. Renée Michelle Gordon's message is timeless and her timing is perfect even though she uses modern technology to get there. I've had a loving marriage for over 20 years. Can't wait to buy copies of this book for my single friends. This book needs to be in the hands of everyone who wants to find their Mr. or Mrs. Right!"

- Valerie Harris
Social Media Expert, Author of Becoming A Time Freedom Freak: Mastering The Art Of Outsourcing For A Thriving Life

"Swipe for Mr. Right is Dr. Renée's gift to the heart. This book is a manual for building genuine connections. I've been married to my love and soulmate over 20 glorious years. Dr. Renée's information in this book should be a mandatory read for anyone seeking to find their everlasting love, creating lasting joy and understanding."

- Kimberly Warren
Vice President Financial Services Regional

As a health and wellness expert happily married for over 27 years, Dr. Love's "Swipe for Mr. Right" orchestrated a love symphony in my life. Her harmonious advice resonates deeply, guiding me to a love that feels authentic and everlasting. This book, a lifeline for those seeking love's true essence, is filled with pearls of wisdom that transformed my outlook. Dr. Renée's insightful questions, like "Who am I 'being' to attract the Love of my Life?" and "Who would I need to be at peace with my past?" are invaluable guides on the journey to a soulful and enduring connection. Grateful for her wisdom.

- Dara McHenry
Health & Wellness Expert

"Swipe for Mr. Right" is an absolute game-changer in the world of online dating and finding your perfect partner. In a time when navigating the digital dating landscape can feel overwhelming, this book offers invaluable insights. Dr. Renée's profound wisdom shines through, emphasizing the importance of self-love as the foundation for building a fulfilling relationship. Her expertise in nurturing and strengthening connections is truly remarkable. If you're ready to embark on a journey towards finding lasting love in the digital age, this book is your compass. Prepare to swipe right on the life you've always dreamed of!

- Rhonda Nyberg
Founder of Renewed with Rhonda, Motivational Speaker and Leadership Coach

"Endlessly grateful for my love and relationship expert, the brilliant mind behind 'Swipe for Mr. Right.' As a high fashion model seeking committed love, her guidance has been transformative. Her book and personalized coaching illuminate the path to lasting love. Thank you for navigating me towards a fulfilling, committed relationship!"

- Rebecca Boerger
Professional Model

"What I love about this book is how Dr. Renée voices all the concerns running round my head about online dating... and then proceeds to answer them. A wonderfully practical approach which I'm enjoying delving into and looking forward to finding my Mr. Right after having done the preparatory work on me first. Gotta be Mrs. Right before I can hope to attract Mr. Right. If you are in the market for a new significant other, this book is just what you need in this modern world of online dating!"

- Wendy Corner
Speaker, Speaker Coach, Best selling Author of Your Words Have Power, TEDx Trainer

"Swipe for Mr. Right by Dr. Renée, is a lifeline for anyone seeking love's true essence. I would highly recommend this book to all of my single friends.

The book's pearls of wisdom transformed my outlook, leading me to a soulful connection." So grateful.

- Claudia Moehring
Licensed Psychologist, Leadership Trainer and Coac

"Dr. Renée's understanding that a single person's strength comes from it's most valuable asset, knowing who they are and who is right for them! Her book teaches the new fundamentals of relationships that every single person desperately wants and needs. This is a must read for those searching for love!"

- Tommy "Lemonade"
Author of When God Gives You Lemons

"If you are serious about finding everlasting love, then you must read and apply the principles, strategies and techniques in this powerful relationship guide book by Dr. Renée Gordon."

- America Wagner
Chief Marketing Officer at Webive/Digital/Greater Chattanooga

Dr. Love's Swipe for Mr. Right is a true masterpiece that goes beyond conventional relationship advice. As a real estate broker navigating the complexities of love, Dr. Renée's book emerged as an invaluable love mentor in my life. The profound impact it had on my relationship journey is immeasurable. Swipe for Mr. Right is more than a book; it's a lifeline for anyone seeking love's true essence. Dr. Renée's exceptional wisdom, woven into its pages, transformed my outlook on love and relationships. This transformative guide led me to a soulful connection, enriching not only my personal life but influencing how I approach and appreciate genuine connections in all aspects of my life. Grateful for the profound impact Dr. Love's insights have had on my journey to authentic and fulfilling love.

- Lecia Westerman
Real Estate Investor & Real Estate Broker

As an Alkaline Water expert and health & wellness coach, happily married for over 10 years, Dr. Love's "Swipe for Mr. Right" is a love design masterpiece. The spectacular advice and coaching from Dr. Renée resonates, guiding me to an authentic and everlasting love. This book, a lifeline for those seeking love's true essence, transformed my outlook and led me to a soulful connection. Grateful for Dr. Renée's wisdom and expert coaching.

- Tony Mack
CEO & Founder, Rainwater Global, LLC

What a fascinating, educational and prescriptive walk through on how to find your significant other in this vast technologically abundant world of dating. I found it hard to put Dr. Renée's book down as with each chapter, she creates a clear picture of what the landscape is while providing the benefits and pitfalls for online dating. Another successful book offering from Dr. Renée for those pursuing love.

- Laila Ansari
Relationship & Leadership Coach. Author of Awaken Your Inner Titan

"Single available people have been waiting for a book like this to come along for a long time. Dr. Renée understands the power of building a strong connection by first loving yourself. Take the first step in your self-love journey and buy this book and learn to attract your ideal life partner!"

- Nicole Pilon Daniel
Financial Consultant with Crawford & Associates, and Essential Oil Junkie and Natural Health Advocate for doTERRA Essential Oils

Who better to guide you on this "the maze of finding true love than the one who created a system that attracted over 3,000 men on match.com to wade through and find her husband from Heaven herself. That would be Dr. Renée. Her book explains the reasons that make her system work and the step by step process to get there. If you want to find real love then read this book and let her guide you in a way to avoid the pitfalls all of us have fallen into and now can avoid.

- Constance-Noelle Hatley
Real Estate Investor & Analyst

"Dr. Renée Michelle Gordon's message is timeless and her timing is perfect even though she uses modern technology to get there. I've been in a very loving and meaningful marriage for over 20 years. This book needs to be in the hands of everyone who wants to find their Mr. or Mrs. Right!"

- Rose Opengart
Author of Find Your Where

"Definitely one of the top thought leaders of our time in the area of building strong, loving relationship and it shows in reading this book and her teachings. We have been married for over 60 phenomenal years and Dr. Renée's wisdom hits a home run after home run as her stories reveal the right way to empower yourself to finding your life partner and ensuring the future of getting happily married!"

- Ann Sherman
Elite Executive National Sales Director of Mary Kay Cosmetics

"Are you afraid that your marriage is in jeopardy because your spouse is not relating to your like they did in the beginning? Swipe for Mr. Right is the solution before it becomes a problem. Understanding the DNA of a single person is key to writing this book. Dr. Renée, bravo, finally someone gets it and is willing to share it with the rest of us single folk!"

- Fran Haynes
"Fragrant Fran" Mary Kay Consultant & Lifestyle Expert

"Dr. Renée Michelle Gordon's message is timeless and her timing is perfect even though she uses modern technology to get there. This book needs to be in the hands of everyone who wants to find their Mr. or Mrs. Right!"

- Peggy Marchese
CEO of Bellissimo Casa, LLC , Property Management Company & MasterSleuth Investigations

"Dr. Renée Michelle Gordon has nailed it with this book. The timing of her wisdom and the knowledge contained in these pages is an excellent guide to those individuals seeking to find their life mate. I've been happily married for over 25 years. I highly recommend Swipe for Mr. Right if you want to create a winning life together!" When my son is ready for a relationship, I will be giving this book to him and all of our single friends.

- Terri Schlabaugh
"Domestic Goddess" & Ranch Management

Dr. Renée's message is life-changing! Not only does her information reflect a need in finding your perfect life mate, but you can tell from her stories that she doesn't just talks the talk, she has walk the walk. I highly recommend this book for any person wanting to improve in their search for love!"

- Bill Collins
Author of Your Grandpa is a KickAss Criminal Attorney

"This book will put you on the high road to relationship success, happy sweetheart and engaged lovers. Do yourself a favor and learn these principles to reap the benefits for your life!

- Joe Buford
Judo Instructor, Marine & Actor

"Dr. Renée walks her talk! From her personable and real stories, you can tell that the author practiced what she preaches, she does it from a compassionate perspective. I love the exercises that puts the learning into action making the book feel like it was written just for you. A must read for any single person wanting to connect with their own soulmate!"

- Ben Carins
Executive Coach

"The old way of "my way of the highway" is dead and obsolete. Create a loving culture that is empathetic, communicative and purposeful. Dr. Renée has given us the tools to make our daily life searching for our Mr. Right elegant and real!"

- Ron Hori
Insurance & Health Advisor

Who better to guide you thro' the maze of finding true love than the one who created a system that attracted over 3,000 men to wade thro' and find her husband from Heaven herself? That would be Dr. Renee. Her book explains the reasons that make her system work & the step-by-step process to get there. If you want to find real love then read this book and let her guide you in a way to avoid the pitfalls all of us have fallen into & now can avoid.

Constance-Noelle Hatley

This sourcebook is dedicated to
my husband, Jim Connolly.

Jim urged me to write it,
and helped shape it.

Without him it would not exist.

Acknowledgements

"Your life is your message to the world, make sure it is inspiring"

- Dr. Renée Gordon

To my husband, Jim Connolly, who has been a driving force in bringing this book to fruition. Thank you for making this book happen. I have been blessed by my soul mate. My best friend, the Chairman of the Board of my company. Thank you for the countless nights you have heard my heart and listened to my fears and dreams and for believing in me.

"You are Powerful"!!! Just step into that space of Power....I hear this all the time from my husband, Jim. He is always encouraging me. Whether I'm finishing writing a book or stepping onto a stage as a keynote speaker. I'm very fortunate to have not only a loving, supportive, brilliant, and handsome husband, but he's also my business partner. WOW!! Did I get lucky. Sometimes I think he can almost "walk on water"… Sometimes I even think he's from another planet or galaxy.

Thank you, Jim.

To the team of EventRaptor and their Principles, Steve & Jennie Eriksen for their loving support, their belief in our mission to find love for people around the world, supportive, their brilliant marketing ideas, suggestions, and implementation systems. To create a huge and spectacular book launch of this project "Swipe for Mr. Right".

Noelle Hepworth - their visionary and creative ideas of formatting and presenting an outstanding book cover that conveys exactly what this project is about. We were impressed the moment we met them.

Lee Pound - I've known him for over 20 years. A brilliant and remarkable mind. Love his steady calmness, patience and literary magic, and consistent excellence.

For my sister, Yvonne for her support and who I wish only the best for her...

To my mother, who taught me how to wrap beautiful breathtaking presents. The "tough" love she taught me helped me create a "thick skin" in business.

To my Auntie Joy, who is my paragon of poise, grace, and style. She cultivated my love for fashion, designer shoes, and elegant living. Her teachings on etiquette and flair in furnishings transformed me. I cherish the memories of the glamorous dinner parties she effortlessly hosted, shaping my appreciation for refined living. Grateful for her enduring influence. She taught me how to create my own fashion style, elegance, and mindfulness.

My Grandmother, Justina. "My cherished Grandmother, Justina, now resting in heaven with my father, shaped the core of who I am. In Hawaii, her hospitality mastery unfolded—cooking, entertaining, and creating events seamlessly. With no recipes, she crafted spectacular moments, from invitations to exquisite tablescapes and gourmet delights. A maestro of no-stress entertaining, she'd say, 'just feel and 'be' with the ingredients.' Her wisdom extends beyond hospitality, guiding my 'Be, Do, & Have' mindset. The space of 'be' she instilled continues to enrich my life. Grateful for her profound teachings and enduring legacy."

My father, Jim Gordon, who is in heaven with my grandmother is looking from the heavens above. Who always gave me encouragement and believed so much in me. My father helped me develop a magnetic personality, self-confidence, respect, leadership, entrepreneurship, enthusiasm, courage, sincerity of purpose, strength of character, persistence, integrity, and determination. He gave me my business acumen as well as advice with the opposite sex. He said, "Never cry over a guy, there's always another one, just like a bus, every five minutes."

Napoleon Hill, is a special mentor, to me. He died before I was even born. I've been following him since I was five years old. His book *Think and Grow Rich* is a personal development adventure in awareness. One of my favorite quotes I implement daily is, "If you want favors, bestow favors." This is in accordance with the law of harmonious attraction through the operation of which, "We get exactly what we give." Another favorite classic quote: "Big pay and little responsibility are circumstances seldom found together." So, your job is to Take Responsibility and succeed anyway!!..

My sales coach, Eric Lofholm. Eric has been my sales coach since 2005. He's taught me the art and science of selling and his system process. To be a sales superstar and to be my own cheerleader. He says "People don't always need advice but rather encouragement."

Another quote from Eric that inspired me to write this book is, "All you need to do is ask yourself what you want, then develop the strategy to achieve this, then take massive action on a daily basis." I practice this daily.

My other sales coach, Jeffery Gitomer, whose teachings have had a profound impact on me. And, his guiding principles of sales mastery.

My mentor and spiritual coach, Niurka. She has guided me through the journey of awakening and self-realization. She taught me to live into this phrase "We create as we speak our words have that much power". And, teaching me the lessons of Neuro-linguistic programming and the Path of Self Mastery.

My manifestation coach, John Assaraf- being in his inner circle for many years I've learned and become more of who I was meant to be in this world. Working with John Assaraf has been life-changing. His expertise as a manifestation and transformational coach is unparalleled. John's insights and guidance have propelled me toward achieving my goals and unlocking untapped potential. With gratitude, I celebrate the positive shifts he has inspired, paving the way for profound transformation and success. Thank you, John, for being a beacon of empowerment on my journey." And, learning how to step into the future and visualize my future before it comes to fruition.

My trainer and nutritionist, Bill Mabry. "Coach Bill," my trainer and nutritionist, is a true lifesaver. Alongside my husband Jim and God, he played a pivotal role in my miraculous recovery from stage 4 cancer a year and a half ago. Bill's expertise and support transformed my health journey. Grateful for his guidance, he's a blessing and an integral part of our dynamic health team. Thank you, Coach Bill, for being instrumental in my healing and well-being." If it weren't for him, my husband Jim, and God, I wouldn't be here today. What a blessing Coach Bill has been in our lives.

Swipe for Mr. Right

Best-Kept Secrets to Attracting Your Love Online

Dr. Renée Michelle Gordon

Foreword by January Donovan
Foreword by Eric Lofholm

Swipe for Mr. Right

Best Kept Secrets to Attracting Your Love Online

©2023 Dr. Renée Michelle Gordon

Published by:
Wisdom Eye Publishing
Chattanooga, TN
www.WisdomEyePublishing.com

All Rights Reserved. No part of this book may be used or reproduced in any manner whatsoever without the express written permission of the author. Address all inquires to:

Dr. Renée Michelle Gordon
www.SwipeforMrRight.com

ISBN: 979-8-9896108-0-8

Editor: Lee Pound
Cover and Interior Layout Design: Noelle Hepworth
Book Project Coordinator & Coach: Jim Connolly
Divine Inspiration: James E. Gordon & God
Every attempt has been made to source properly all quotes.
Printed in the United States of America

Disclaimer

The purpose of this book is to educate and entertain. Neither the author nor publisher guarantees that anyone following the ideas, time, suggestions, techniques, or strategies within it will become successful. The author and publisher shall have neither liability nor responsibility to anyone with respect to any loss or damage caused, or alleged to be caused, directly or indirectly, by the information contained in this book.

Table of Contents

Introduction	35
Foreword by January Donovan	41
Foreword by Eric Lofholm	45
Preface	51
The Allure of Finding Mr. Right on Online Dating Websites	57
Knowing Yourself	87
Knowing What You Want	109
Designing Your Profile	143
Launching Your Profile	155
Following Up	171
Closing the Deal	195
The Transition	211

Why Not Educate, Engage & Inspire Your Next Audience?

Speaking, Online Courses, Workshops & Coaching

If you'd like Dr. Renée to speak at your next event, contact her team to check her available dates.

Sample Speaking/Workshop Topics:

- *Pros & Cons of Dating in the Workplace or Business*
- *Finding Your Love in a Busy Lifestyle*
- *Attract Your Soulmate in 90 Days or Less*
- *Learn What a 75 Year Socio-Scientific Study Tells Us About Our Happiness*
- *Swipe for Mr. Right, Best-Kept Secrets to Attracting Your Love Online*

www.SwipeforMrRight.com

www.ReneeLoveCoach.com

www.Reneegordonspeaker.com

Swipe for Mr. Right

Swipe for Mr. Right

Introduction

Swipe for Mr. Right - Best-Kept Secrets to Attracting Your Love Online

In the fast-paced digital landscape of the 21st century, the quest for love has taken a new and exciting turn: online dating. In "Swipe for Mr. Right," we embark on a journey through the intricate world of online dating, unraveling the secrets to attracting genuine love in a realm often characterized by quick swipes and fleeting connections.

Chapter 1: The Allure of Finding Mr. Right on Online Dating Websites

Online dating has become the modern arena for seekers of love, a vast landscape where connections are formed with a simple swipe. This chapter delves into the allure of this digital realm, exploring the possibilities and challenges it presents. From the convenience of swiping through profiles to the potential for meaningful connections, we unravel the essence of finding Mr. Right in the vast sea of online dating.

Chapter 2: Knowing Yourself

The foundation of any successful relationship lies in self-awareness. Chapter 2 emphasizes the importance of introspection and self-discovery. To attract Mr. Right, you must first know yourself – your values, aspirations, and the essence of your being. Through insightful exercises and reflections, this chapter guides you on a journey of self-discovery that will not only enhance your profile but also set the stage for a genuine connection.

Chapter 3: Knowing What You Want

Clarifying your desires is a crucial step on the path to finding Mr. Right. Chapter 3 delves into the art of knowing what you want in a partner. From deal-breakers to must-haves, we navigate the landscape of your desires and help you create a blueprint for the ideal relationship. Understanding your preferences is essential for attracting the right match and fostering a connection that aligns with your long-term goals.

Chapter 4: Designing Your Profile

Your online profile is your digital first impression. Chapter 4 focuses on the art of designing a compelling profile that reflects the authentic you. From choosing the right photos to crafting an engaging bio, we provide tips and tricks to make your profile stand out amidst the digital crowd. A well-crafted profile is the key to attracting the attention of potential Mr. Rights and initiating meaningful conversations.

Chapter 5: Launching Your Profile

With your profile in hand, it's time to take the plunge. Chapter 5 guides you through the process of launching your profile into the online dating sphere. From selecting the right platform to navigating the intricacies of online communication, we provide practical advice on making a memorable entrance into the world of digital dating.

Chapter 6: Following Up

Building connections is an ongoing process. Chapter 6 delves into the art of following up – from initiating conversations to maintaining engagement. We explore effective communication strategies that go beyond the initial swipe, helping you build rapport and establish a foundation for a potential connection with Mr. Right.

Chapter 7: Closing the Deal

As connections deepen, the time comes to explore the potential for a meaningful relationship. Chapter 7 navigates the delicate art of closing the deal – transitioning from digital interactions to real-life connections. From arranging the first date to navigating the complexities of virtual to real-world dynamics, we provide insights to help you smoothly transition from online connection to offline reality.

Chapter 8: The Transition

The final chapter explores the transition from dating to a committed relationship. Navigating this phase requires careful consideration and communication. Chapter 8 guides you through the intricacies of the transition, offering insights on establishing a deeper connection and navigating the exciting yet challenging journey towards a long-lasting relationship.

In "Swipe for Mr. Right," we unravel the secrets, strategies, and nuances of online dating, providing you with a roadmap to navigate this ever-evolving landscape.

Whether you're a newcomer to digital dating or a seasoned swiper, this book offers practical advice, heartfelt insights, and a wealth of knowledge to empower you in your quest for Mr. Right in the digital age. Get ready to swipe with purpose and embark on a journey to discover lasting love in the world of online connections.

FOREWORD

January Donovan

To those that seek a love that fulfills the depth of your soul:

It is with deep joy and anticipation that I welcome you to the timeless and powerful wisdom encapsulated within the pages of "Swipe for Mr. Right: Best Kept Secrets to Attracting Your Love Online." As the founder of The Wholeness Coaching School and The Woman School, a practical life training on how to be a woman of value in a time of confusion, I find this book inspiring in its depth, but also in its practical application. I've dedicated my life to helping individuals discover their inner strength, embrace their uniqueness, and unlock the doors to the love that they deserve, and I can say this book will serve as your compass in navigating the tumultuous dating world. Everyone on the online dating world should use this book.

In a world where digital connections have become part of the fabric of finding authentic love, you have to raise your standards and guard your values while creating pathways to profound connections. You have to resist settling and compromising on the love you deserve. Each swipe holds the potential to lead you closer to the love you seek, and in the vast landscape of online dating, every interaction is an opportunity to unveil the best version of you. This book will equip you with the tools you need to honor what you deeply desire.

The key to attracting your Mr. Right lies not just in the algorithms of dating apps but in honoring your sacred value. It is a journey that goes beyond the surface, beyond the carefully curated profiles and charming bios, it has to be rooted in self love that begins with self awareness. This book is a guide to help you unravel the complexities of online dating while empowering you to cultivate your unique and authentic self, and attract the love you seek.

To achieve great love, you have to honor your self worth, embrace your strength, weakness and vulnerabilities. You cannot simply conform to societal expectations. As you embark on this journey, remember that the power to attract the right love begins within you.

"Swipe for Mr. Right" is not just a manual for online dating; it's a mirror reflecting the extraordinary woman within you, beckoning her to step into the spotlight and design her own love story.

Within these pages, you'll discover the best-kept secrets to navigating the world of online dating with grace, authenticity, and a deep sense of self-worth. Whether you're a seasoned swiper or stepping into the digital dating arena for the first time, the insights and revelations shared in this book will be your guiding wisdom.

Love, in its truest form, is not about settling; it's about aligning with a partner who celebrates the fullness of who you are, and complements your journey. This book is a testament to the belief that every woman deserves a love that sees her, respects her, and elevates her spirit to be fully alive. It's a celebration of the unwavering worth that resides within you, guiding you to attract a love that mirrors the love you have for yourself.

As you immerse yourself in the wisdom and guidance contained in "Swipe for Mr. Right," let it be a reminder that the journey to love is not a sprint but a dance – a dance that can last a lifetime. You deserve a love that inspires you and cherishes you for all that you are and all that you could be.

May your swipes be intentional, your heart open, and may your love story unfold far greater than you have ever imagined.

With Love & Encouragement,

January Donovan
Founder, The Wholeness Coaching School &
The Woman School

FOREWORD
Eric Lofholm

Welcome to the thrilling journey of "Swipe for Mr. Right," a book that transcends the conventional realms of dating and relationships.

As the founder of a sales training company, I've spent my career honing the art of persuasion, negotiation, and human connection. Little did I know that the principles I've mastered in the boardroom would find their way into the most intimate aspects of my life – my quest for love.

In the world of sales, success hinges on understanding your audience, identifying their needs, and building authentic connections. The parallels between the sales arena and the dating landscape are uncanny. In both realms, the art of swiping – be it through a touchscreen or a crowded room –

has become a contemporary ritual, a dance of possibilities where we navigate the intricate steps of human interaction.

Allow me to introduce myself. I am not just a sales guru; I am a man who found his "Queen" through the digital dance of swipes and clicks. My beloved wife has been my anchor, my confidante, and my inspiration. She is the reason I approach life, both personal and professional, with a mindset of abundance and the unwavering belief that the right match is out there for each of us.

As you embark on the pages of "Swipe for Mr. Right," prepare to be enlightened, entertained, and, most importantly, empowered. This isn't just a guide to mastering the art of swiping; it's a roadmap to self-discovery and understanding the dynamics of modern love. Swipe right for the potential within yourself and the limitless possibilities that lie in the connections you make.

The digital age has revolutionized the way we connect with others, introducing a myriad of possibilities that were once confined to the realms of serendipity. In a world where the swipe of a finger can open the door to romance, it's crucial to navigate with intention and authenticity. This book is not just a collection of tips and tricks; it's a philosophy that underscores the importance of being true to yourself while actively seeking the partner who complements your journey.

In my years of coaching individuals in the art of selling, I've come to understand the importance of aligning values, communicating effectively, and creating win-win scenarios. These principles are not exclusive to the sales pitch; they are the very foundation of meaningful relationships. "Swipe for Mr. Right" will guide you through the nuances of modern dating, helping you craft a compelling narrative that attracts the right match while staying true to your authentic self.

As you delve into the chapters ahead, remember that the journey to finding Mr. Right is not just about finding a partner – it's about discovering the best version of yourself. It's about embracing vulnerability, celebrating individuality, and recognizing that love, much like a successful sale, is a collaborative endeavor.

So, fasten your seatbelt and get ready to embark on a transformative expedition. "Swipe for Mr. Right" isn't just a book; it's a companion on your journey to love and self-discovery. May your swipes be purposeful, your connections profound, and your love story be nothing short of extraordinary.

Here's to finding your Mr. Right in the digital age, and may your love story be as legendary as the one I continue to write with my "Queen Heather".

Warm regards,

Eric Lofholm
President Eric Lofholm International

Author of Continuous Sales Improvement, The System & many other sales books...

PREFACE
Navigating the Digital Landscape of Love

In the realm of love, some narratives unfold against the backdrop of extraordinary events that redefine the very essence of our existence. As the author of "Swipe for Mr. Right," I invite you to embark on a journey woven with threads of resilience, revelation, and the profound wisdom born from two near-death experiences that shaped the trajectory of my life.

The odyssey began with a tragic car accident that claimed the life of my father and left me in a coma for an unfathomable nine-and-a-half months. In that suspended animation between life and the ethereal, I wrestled with the fragility of existence. Emerging from that cocoon, I carried forth a profound revelation: life, with all its uncertainties, is a tapestry meant to be woven with purpose and meaning.

This wisdom became the compass guiding the narrative of "Swipe for Mr. Right." As I emerged from the shadows of my own near-death encounters, I found myself traversing a world increasingly shaped by digital connections. The rise of online dating platforms unfolded before me, a landscape where individuals sought companionship, connection, and perhaps, true love. Amidst this sea of swipes, I discerned the potential for genuine connections and the peril of trivial pursuits.

"Swipe for Mr. Right" is more than a guide to navigating the complexities of online dating—it is a testament to the belief that life is too precious to be squandered on transient encounters and meaningless liaisons. My brushes with mortality underscored the profound truth that time is a nonrenewable resource—a finite currency to be spent wisely. This realization, etched into the very fabric of my being, forms the heartbeat of this book.

As we embark on this exploration together, I invite you to consider the depth of your desires, the authenticity of your connections, and the sacredness of time. This book is not merely a compendium of strategies but a narrative woven with the threads of vulnerability, resilience, and the profound wisdom that life's most cherished moments often emerge from the union of two beating hearts.

In sharing this journey, I bear witness to the transformative power of online connections. For in the digital ether, I found my own Mr. Right—an enduring love that has stood the test of over 23 years. Our story is not just an anecdote; it is a testament to the profound potential of online dating. It is with a heart brimming with joy that I extend the possibility of such happiness to you.

As we navigate the labyrinth of online dating together, let these pages be a compass guiding you through the digital wilderness, navigating the contours of meaningful connections, and helping you uncover the hidden secrets to attracting your Mr. Right online. May you find, as I did, that love in the swipe era is not just a possibility but a reality waiting to be embraced. Welcome to "Swipe for Mr. Right," a journey into the heart of intentional and lasting love.

With Gratitude & Love,

Dr. Renée Gordon

CHAPTER 1

The Allure of Finding Mr. Right on Online Dating Websites

"Have confidence in yourself that you can do whatever it is you truly believe in."

— *Dr. Renée Gordon*

- ♥ Why is everyone fixated on finding their Mr. Right on an online dating website?
- ♥ Can this dating process be used for casual dating or is it only reserved for long term relationships?
- ♥ What is online dating for long-term relationships?
- ♥ What are the advantages of using internet dating sites as a search tool?
- ♥ What are the downfalls of using internet dating sites as a search tool?
- ♥ How soon do I get started once I begin reading this book?
- ♥ What if I still have lots of fears or anxiousness towards attracting my dream man due to past relationship failures?
- ♥ Is searching for my Mr. Right by way of using an online dating site easy?
- ♥ What other things should I be aware of about online dating that most people don't talk about?
- ♥ What can you relate the online dating process to?

Why is everyone fixated on finding their Mr. Right on an online dating website?

In the digital age, online dating has become a prevalent avenue for individuals to seek out their romantic partners. The notion of finding Mr. Right, the perfect life partner, has captivated the minds and hearts of countless people who turn to online dating websites in hopes of discovering a meaningful and lasting connection. Why is everyone fixated on this modern approach to romance? This question is multifaceted, encompassing various factors that contribute to the widespread appeal of online dating in the quest for Mr. Right.

> *The first question my clients ask when we begin their search through my Mr. Right attraction process is, "When do we go online at a dating site?"*

These powerful tools, with their vast databases of available potential suitors, put you in front of many people you may not otherwise meet. I not only help people use these many online dating apps to help them find their own Mr. or Mrs. Right, but this is how I found my own life mate. I am a believer! More on my love journey later.

Convenience and Accessibility

Online dating platforms offer unparalleled convenience and accessibility. In a fast-paced world where people juggle demanding careers, personal commitments, and social lives, the ability to connect with potential partners from the comfort of one's home or smartphone is undeniably appealing. The 24/7 availability of online dating websites allows individuals to explore their options at their own pace, without the constraints of time or location.

One of my newer clients, we'll call him Mr. V, is a very busy high-tech executive. The convenience of putting himself out there to test the dating market when he has spare time after his work day makes online dating a great way to begin his search for his Mrs. Right.

Diverse Dating Pool

Online dating platforms host an extensive, diverse dating pool, expanding the possibilities of finding a compatible partner. These websites attract people from various backgrounds, professions, and interests, making it easier to meet individuals with whom one shares common values and aspirations. The sheer number of potential matches can increase the likelihood of finding someone who aligns with your vision of Mr. Right.

Later, you'll understand how our process helps you quickly refine your perfect Mr. Right so you can shrink that pool of vast diversity to a pool of possibilities.

Compatibility Algorithms

Many online dating websites employ sophisticated algorithms to match users based on compatibility factors such as personality traits, interests, and values. These algorithms aim to streamline the dating process by presenting users with profiles that are more likely to be a good fit. The promise of science-backed matchmaking adds a layer of confidence for users in their pursuit of Mr. or Mrs. Right.

One client, who got lazy with doing their love coaching homework, ignored our process and relied solely on one dating website that touted a guaranteed love match. At the beginning, their dates were fun and filled with activities that they both enjoyed. After three months, many events, including high holidays, birthdays and even a death in one of the families, showed up on their calendars. The pressure on this couple caused them to slowly break away from each other. What began with common hobbies and interests met its eventual end.

As convenient as having the support of a compatibility algorithm helps in the searching department, understanding how to use these algorithms to your advantage is key.

Filtered Selection Process

Online dating allows users to specify their preferences and deal-breakers, enabling a filtered selection process. You can screen potential partners based on your specific criteria, whether it's age, location, interests, or other factors. This level of customization empowers users to focus their efforts on individuals who are more likely to meet their expectations.

Expanded Social Circles

Online dating extends one's social circles beyond their immediate geographical location. It enables connections with people they might not cross paths with in their everyday lives. This opens new opportunities to meet a unique and special person who could be their Mr. Right.

Anonymity and Reduced Pressure

The virtual nature of online dating provides a level of anonymity that can alleviate the pressure and anxiety often associated with traditional dating. This encourages individuals to be more open, honest, and vulnerable, which fosters deeper connections and potentially leads to the discovery of Mr. Right.

Time to Get to Know Each Other

Online dating allows individuals to engage in extended conversations before meeting in person. This extra time provides an opportunity to get to know each other's personalities, values, and life goals more thoroughly. It can lead to a stronger emotional connection when Mr. Right is finally found.

Expanding Horizons

Online dating encourages people to step outside their comfort zones and explore relationships with individuals they might not have otherwise considered. This can lead to personal growth and a deeper understanding of one's own desires and needs in a partner, ultimately aiding in the search for Mr. Right.

Reduced Stigma

The stigma once associated with online dating has significantly diminished over the years. It has become a socially accepted and normalized way to meet potential partners. This shift has encouraged more people to try online dating as a legitimate avenue for finding love and happiness.

Success Stories

Online dating has produced numerous success stories where individuals find their Mr. Right and build lasting relationships. These stories serve as inspiration and proof that meaningful connections can indeed be forged in the digital realm, motivating others to embark on their own online dating journey.

Varied Expectations

While some individuals use online dating platforms with the sole intent of finding their life partner, others may have different expectations, such as seeking casual dating or friendship. This diverse range of intentions means that online dating caters to a broad spectrum of relationship goals, making it adaptable to individual preferences.

Changing Societal Norms

Societal norms around dating and relationships have evolved. The idea of finding Mr. Right is no longer solely tied to the traditional concept of marriage. People now seek partners who fulfill emotional, intellectual, and personal needs, and online dating aligns with these changing dynamics.

Avenues for Self-Discovery

The journey to find Mr. Right often involves self-discovery. Online dating provides an opportunity for individuals to reflect on their own desires, values, and aspirations in a partner. This introspection can be a valuable part of the process.

The fixation on finding Mr. Right on online dating websites can be attributed to the convenience, accessibility, and promise of tailored matchmaking. The appeal lies in the opportunity to connect with a diverse dating pool, employ advanced algorithms, and customize the selection process. Moreover, online dating offers anonymity, reduced pressure, and the chance to expand horizons, making it a compelling option for those in search of meaningful, lasting relationships. As societal norms continue to evolve, online dating remains a prominent and adaptable avenue for individuals to explore their desires, connect with others, and ultimately find their own version of Mr. Right.

Can this dating process be used for casual dating or is it only reserved for long term relationships?

Online dating has revolutionized the way people meet and connect, offering a platform for a wide range of relationship goals. While many individuals turn to online dating with the hope of finding a long-term partner, it's essential to recognize that the online dating process can be used for casual dating as well. The versatility of online dating means it caters to a spectrum of preferences and intentions, whether a brief fling or a lifetime commitment.

There's a common misconception that online dating platforms are solely meant for individuals searching for their future spouse. However, this notion doesn't reflect the diverse array of desires and needs that people have when it comes to romantic relationships.

Online dating provides a convenient, efficient way to meet people with similar interests for casual dating. It's particularly popular among those who want to explore various connections without the pressure of commitment.

What is Online Dating for Long-Term Relationships?

On the other end of the spectrum, people also use online dating with the primary goal of finding a life partner. Online dating provides several advantages for those seeking long-term relationships:

1. Compatibility Matching: Many dating platforms use advanced algorithms to match individuals based on their compatibility in terms of personality, interests, and values, enhancing the chances of finding a compatible long-term partner.

2. Profile Details: Online dating profiles often contain comprehensive information about a person's background, interests, and goals, enabling individuals to assess potential compatibility before making a commitment.

3. Communication and Connection: Online dating offers a space for meaningful conversations and getting to know someone deeply, which is essential for establishing a strong foundation for a long-term relationship.

4. Increased Opportunities: Online dating expands your reach, connecting you with a wider pool of potential partners and increasing the chances of finding someone with whom you can build a life together.

5. Safety and Screening: Online dating allows individuals to screen potential partners and communicate in a secure, controlled environment, making it easier to protect themselves and their interests.

What are the advantages of using internet dating sites as a search tool?

The digital age has transformed every aspect of our lives, including the way we find love. Internet dating sites have become powerful tools for singles seeking meaningful connections. The advantages of using these platforms are numerous and continue to redefine how we approach dating. Online dating has even improved how we make our initial one on one connection. Before, maybe a brief phone call or text was our first personal contact. Now, in addition to phone and text, we have face to face virtual tools like Zoom (we all know how instrumental this was in staying productive during the Pandemic), Team, FaceTime and others. I like to think that we have an advantage over the dawn of internet dating which I'll discuss later in this book.

Broadening Horizons

Internet dating sites break down geographical barriers. They connect individuals from different cities, states, and even countries. This expands your dating pool, increasing the chances of finding a compatible partner who might not have otherwise crossed your path. When I was single, I believed that it was very beneficial to create a lot of specific details about the person I wanted to attract into my life. I called this idea "Love by Design!". When you get very specific like this, you shrink your pool of possible suitors or prospects. This is why you should think about expanding your geographical barriers accordingly.

Convenience and Accessibility

One of the most significant advantages of online dating is convenience. You can search for potential matches anytime, anywhere, and at your own pace. This flexibility suits the busy lives many people lead, making it easier to balance work, social commitments, and the quest for love. But like anything you commit to, staying on top of the action makes it more convenient as in the "inch by inch is a cinch" mindset.

Detailed Profiles

Internet dating sites offer detailed profiles, allowing you to learn more about potential partners before making contact. You see photos and read about their interests, values, and lifestyle choices, making it easier to assess compatibility. Of course, examining their heart by reaching into their soul is part of the process after the initial meeting. More on that later.

Compatibility Matching

Many dating sites employ sophisticated algorithms that match users based on compatibility factors such as personality traits, values, and interests. These algorithms can significantly increase the chances of finding a compatible partner who shares your long-term goals. I like any tool that helps you evaluate a potential suitor up front. Eliminate the "Never" characteristics like, don't smoke, don't drink, and don't take showers (you think I'm kidding, it has happened, fear of frequent showers). This helps you refine your search more easily using algorithms to do your elimination work upfront.

Clear Intentions

Most people use dating sites for a purpose - to find a potential partner. This clarity of intention reduces the uncertainty often present in traditional dating scenarios, where it's not always clear who is looking for a relationship and who is not.

Safety Precautions

Dating sites often include safety features such as user verification and reporting mechanisms to help ensure a safer dating experience. These platforms have taken steps to address concerns about fraudulent profiles and online security. This is the right step to add safety to this process. I still warn my clients that until you've vetted a person yourself, keep a cushion of security between you and the many strangers that you open yourself up to while going through the dating process. I don't want to scare you into non-action in dating, but I do want you to be aware.

Self-Discovery

Online dating can also be a journey of self-discovery. Filling out a profile about who you are and who are you looking for in your life is the fastest way to show that you are ready, a huge advantage in the process of preparing for your Mr. Right. If you are unprepared, as you interact with potential partners and learn about their preferences you may gain a deeper understanding of your own desires and the kind of relationship you truly seek. I want you to prepare more in advance and not wait to self-discover after you joined a dating website. You want to take the reigns as you choose who to attract into your life.

Lower Pressure

The online dating process can be more relaxed than traditional dating, allowing you to take your time and develop connections at your own pace. This lower pressure environment can be particularly appealing for those who might be shy or apprehensive about dating.

Positive Outcomes

Countless successful love stories have originated from internet dating sites. These platforms have brought many of my clients together, fostering meaningful relationships, marriages, and families. I have said many times to my husband Jim, (we've been together for over 23 years) that if it wasn't for the magic of online exposure, we may have never met. He encouraged me to write my first book, Finding Your Love at Last, because it was based on the process that I created while finding love for myself. I might have never written this book if hadn't written that first book. So many glorious things have happened because I listened to my lifelong friend Terry and his wife Kathy, who encouraged me to join the same dating website where they found each other and got married (another positive outcome). Sometimes the media sensationalizes the negative stories that come from people who made poor decisions using online dating apps. By far, more positive outcomes have been produced because of its existence.

Internet dating sites offer a host of advantages that make the search for love more accessible, convenient, and tailored to individual preferences. From broadening your horizons to facilitating compatibility matching and enhancing communication, these platforms have become invaluable tools for those seeking meaningful connections in the digital age. However, it's essential to approach online dating with caution, honesty, and an open heart to unlock its full potential. This is why I created this book as a guide to best use this online dating tool.

What are the downfalls of using internet dating sites as a search tool?

I want to be completely transparent to the pitfalls of internet dating and navigating its challenges. Internet dating sites have undoubtedly transformed the dating landscape, offering a convenient platform to meet potential partners. While these platforms come with numerous advantages, it's crucial to be aware of the potential downfalls that can accompany online dating if you don't prepare yourself. Here are some of the common challenges and pitfalls associated with using internet dating sites as a search tool:

Misrepresentation

Catfishing is a term for a person who pretends to be someone else online. A catfish uses fake photos, and sometimes a false persona, to find friends or romantic partners on the internet. One of the most significant concerns in online dating is the potential for misrepresentation. Some users may post outdated or heavily edited photos, exaggerate their accomplishments, or even create entirely fictional profiles. This can lead to disappointment and frustration when you discover the discrepancies between the online persona and the real person.

When Jim and I first connected online, we spent almost two months talking on the phone with each other before seeing each other face to face. My husband saw my profile pictures on my dating site, but he didn't have a profile on that site. He gave me the URL of his business and told me that I could learn all about him, see pictures and even watch video of him on his website. After talking on the phone for an average of two to three hours per day (sometimes longer on weekends!), he mentioned to me that he was traveling to Southern California in a week and wanted to meet with me. Our relationship was built upon a solid understanding of who we were from the questions that I outlined for him to answer (more on this later). I felt our lives were an open book so getting to meet with him was perfect. He said to me, "How about I call you when I complete my business in town so we can plan something fun together."

When he called me, I told him, "I hope after all of this time talking to you over the phone, you're not planning to take me to a lame coffee date." Of course he knew better and had made plans to have brunch, my favorite meal, at the Loews Santa Monica Beach Hotel, where he was staying. As we firmed up our plans, I asked him, "How will I know you?" You see, I hadn't written down his URL correctly and forgot to ask him for it the next time that we talked. After a while, it didn't seem important because I was connecting with his heart and didn't think about what he looked like until now. I told him, "I don't care if you're short, fat and bald, I know I'll like you just the same."

Jim was a bit surprised by that statement, which put him on guard from his perspective. He started to think that maybe I wasn't who I said I was, and this was an elaborate scheme for me to make him care for me even though I wasn't the person in my photos. Luckily, he took a chance and showed up at the brunch anyway. I think he did admit that he hid behind a marble column just in case until he confirmed I was really me. When I got to the hostess desk of the Loews Hotel restaurant, I asked if Mr. Connolly was here. She then indicated that he was and was standing right behind me. To my pleasure, there was my future husband, all 6'2" athletic and full salt and pepper head of hair of him. I think we were both grateful that there was no misrepresentation.

Overwhelming Choices

The abundance of choices on dating sites can be overwhelming. The paradox of choice can lead to decision fatigue, making it challenging to commit to a single person when there is a perception that someone better may be just one click away. That is why you are here now. You know that online dating can be a great tool to find your perfect Mr. Right but the overwhelming number of choices can be too much. This is why our process, if you follow it, will help you eliminate all those Mr. Wrongs before you ever meet them. For the ones who got through your first line of defense, you have back-up defenses. In other words, you need the right mindset at the beginning before you're thrown into the deep end of the pool of dating That is part of our plan for you, to be prepared.

Superficiality

Online dating often places an emphasis on physical appearance and first impressions. While these factors are undoubtedly essential, they may overshadow other significant qualities, such as personality and shared interests, leading to superficial judgments. However, appearance is part of the equation. My husband Jim said that my headline, Ex-model/Chef pulled him into my profile. Then my headshots and photos got him more interested. But what made him act was reading my profile. He said it was genuine and different. Superficiality is always going to be a big part of dating, online or in person. Look your best for who you are but don't be something you're not. Remember, it only takes that one perfect person to become your Mr. Right. It's not a popularity contest, it's about attracting your perfect life mate, who will be attracted to you for you being you.

Because of the potential for superficiality on online dating, you run the risk of being ghosted and ignored. Some people get so pulled into overwhelm that they react to the next pretty picture that comes along. Obviously, they had not read this book, but you have. Don't worry about them anyway. They may have seemed to be a perfect match, but the universe thought differently. If you do get ghosted, it's probably for the best.

High Expectations

The anonymity and curated profiles on dating sites can sometimes lead to unrealistic expectations. Individuals may expect perfection or an instant connection, which can set them up for disappointment when the real person doesn't match the idealized online image. This is why when we get you up online, you are much more prepared than the average person. Remember, this is a tool, not the sole key to your relationship happiness. Be aware that the sheer volume of people you open yourself up to can be overwhelming and that could cause you or the other to have unrealistic expectations. If that happens, remember that this one was not right for you. It's not about you. Just move on and enjoy the ride.

Addiction and Time Consumption

Finally, for some individuals, online dating can become addictive and time-consuming, especially if they have an addictive personality. Constantly checking messages and profiles can detract from other aspects of life, including work, social activities, and self-care. It's important to check in with yourself and realize that this is just a tool that you can choose to turn on or off at any given time. Your destiny is totally in your hands, Missing a message or one or two minutes more online will not make a difference. Your Mr. Right will be attracted to you no matter what.

How soon do I get started once I begin reading this book?

This book is designed as a learn and do-as-you-go type book. After you complete chapters one and two, you jump into it as soon as you'd like to. One exception though. If during the process of completing chapter two some old baggage rears its ugly head, I suggest you take care of it sooner than later. If that old baggage is preventing you from helping you attract the man of your dreams, then this is the perfect time to clean it up.

I suggest that you talk to your own relationship or life coach to clean it up. If you don't have a coach, there is contact information in this book so you can connect with me for a no obligation, complimentary session.

The Allure of Finding Mr. Right on Online Dating Websites

The fact that you are reading this book is a clear indication that you are ready. Rather than take the traditional approach of "Ready, Set, and Go", we will cut to the chase and simplify the process to "Ready, Go!" We will employ the method that made Silicon Valley famous in that we know that bugs and issues will show up during your online experience. We'll work them out as we proceed through your process of attracting Mr. Right.

This next story shows what I've experienced with my clients for the past five years and is why I wrote this book. We are a society that wants it now. No amount of convincing will show you why it's best to prepare yourself first to avoid repeating old, unsuccessful patterns. So here we go.

My client, we'll call her Tori, came to me headstrong and determined to find her own Mr. Right. She proclaimed that she is not a "dating kind of gal" and is a wife looking for a husband. I admired her conviction to reach her goal but needed to slow her down. Tori had already put up her profile online with unflattering headshots, a rushed personal description and barely any thought towards who she really wanted to attract.

The good news is that she did get hits and they were all a poor match. Since she had experienced the imperfect way of approaching a dating app, she was ready to listen.

I hope that this is you and why you've picked up this book for yourself. Failure only occurs when you give up. Congratulations. You got started, but in the wrong direction. Let's read on and rectify that now.

What if I still have lots of fears or anxiousness towards attracting my dream man due to past relationship failures?

Yes, then you need to clean up. But before you run out to chat with your therapist, complete the next couple of chapters first. Attracting Mr. Wrong over and over can prevent you from going forward again and make you gun shy. I went through the same thing. Remember, what we put out to the universe will continually come back to you. This is why after my failed ninth marriage proposal I began looking at myself and not the person who I kept attracting. When I took personal responsibility for my own actions and attractions, I began to make better choices. I began attracting more of what was truly important to me. All those people that I was engaged to get married to are still wonderful people as I was still a wonderful person, too. I just know that it would have been disastrous if I had continued a life with any of them at this point.

We will focus on this later in this book but be aware that there is hope. You're not doomed to being alone in life. Remember, if I can overcome some of my own monumental, close to getting married for the wrong reasons, mistakes, you can too.

The Allure of Finding Mr. Right on Online Dating Websites

Is searching for my Mr. Right by using an online dating site easy?

Yes and no…

The quest for love and the search for Mr. Right have evolved dramatically in the digital age, with online dating sites providing new avenues for singles to explore potential connections. While these platforms offer convenience and access to a vast pool of potential partners, the ease of finding Mr. Right varies from person to person and comes with its unique set of challenges.

The Perceived Ease

Online dating sites are designed to make the initial steps of finding a partner as straightforward as possible. They offer user-friendly interfaces, advanced search filters, and compatibility algorithms that can help narrow down potential matches. These features are meant to simplify the process and, in many cases, can make it seem relatively easy. But one factor that contributes to the perception of ease in online dating is the abundance of choices. Dating sites provide a broad spectrum of potential partners, allowing users to specify their preferences and search for individuals who align with their values, interests, and relationship goals. The variety of options can make it feel like finding Mr. Right should be within reach.

While online dating sites offer convenience and an extensive selection of potential partners, finding Mr. Right is not without its challenges. Here are some factors to consider. Be clear who your ideal match is when setting up your filtering through profiles. Knowing yourself and knowing your perfect match takes preparation and soul searching but will make your journey easier. The sheer number of profiles on dating sites can be overwhelming. To find Mr. Right, users often need to sift through numerous profiles, which can be time-consuming and mentally exhausting.

As mentioned earlier, misrepresentation can be tough. Not all users on dating sites are completely honest. Some may misrepresent themselves through outdated photos, embellished profiles, or dishonest intentions. This can make it challenging to discern who is genuinely compatible.

Compatibility is complex. While compatibility algorithms are useful tools, they cannot account for the complexity of human relationships. Finding a true connection involves factors beyond what you can quantify in a questionnaire.

Overcoming hurdles in the initial stages of online dating, such as crafting an engaging profile and writing compelling messages, may not be easy for everyone. It can take time and effort to master these skills and make a positive first impression. This is why I wrote this book, to help you systematically write a compelling profile that represents you and the person you seek. I usually tell my clients to follow the process and not get ahead of themselves.

Managing high expectations can be a double-edged sword. While optimism is essential, having unrealistic expectations of finding Mr. Right immediately can lead to disappointment and frustration. That's why it's important to believe that your Mr. Right will appear when he is supposed to appear and meanwhile, keep doing the work.

This will also help you navigate rejection and disappointments, which are part of the online dating experience. Not every connection will lead to a meaningful relationship. Learning to navigate these setbacks is crucial. That's why it's better to learn to love yourself first and attract your Mr. Right later.

Finally, online dating, like traditional dating, can be time-consuming. Building a meaningful connection takes time, patience, and effort. But if you ask anyone who found their Mr. Right (or Mrs. Right), "Was it worth the time looking?" They will ask you, "What time?" In other words, time is inconsequential when being present and attracting your ideal mate.

The ease of finding Mr. Right on an online dating site is a subjective experience that depends on individual factors including preferences, communication skills, and patience. While these platforms offer a convenient way to meet potential partners, the path to finding a true and lasting connection is rarely without its challenges. It's essential for individuals to approach online dating with a balanced perspective, realistic expectations, and a commitment to the journey of finding love. With the right mindset and effort, online dating can be a viable and accessible route to discovering Mr. Right.

What other things should I be aware of about online dating that most people don't talk about?

Besides devoting time daily to the process, remember the follow-up. Most people get sucked into the bevy of headshots that run rampant in their minds at the beginning of the search process. Once we get over this feeding frenzy condition, we can settle into what is important to us. This is why later in this book we share with you how to pace yourself during this process. Eventually, you will need to follow up on some of the connections you're making. The key is to go with your gut, look over their profiles, send a message, then forget about it. If it's meant to be, they will follow up. Remember, all those people on the online dating site that you've chosen are looking too. They may be half into getting to know someone and don't want to become distracted. It may be a while before they get back to you.

When you do make a connection by following our process, you can quickly evaluate whether they make the cut. I like to think of this part as like the game we used to play when we were kids called Stop Light.

Stop Light was a group game that involved a lead person in the front that would say either, "Green light, yellow light or stop light." The purpose of the game is to reach the lead person position first while still following the rules. Say for instance, the person says, "green light" and then immediately yells out "yellow light." If you didn't slow down when you heard "yellow light,", you were sent back to the beginning.

When you're dating online, every step of the way is met with red lights, yellow lights, and green lights. This helps you stay within the process and not get too caught up emotionally. Most people don't talk about this very difficult part of the process. Look at online dating as a game at first. Don't get too caught up with your feelings. Look at it like great advertising to get you out there in the dating process. Play it cool and be cool until you know for sure. More on that later in this book.

What can you relate the online dating process to?

I've alluded to this earlier as a game or a process. For those who are entrepreneurs, look at it like acquiring a business. At first, I created this original process for me. I needed to find a way to look for my own Mr. Right differently than I was doing it previously. I knew if I kept doing the same thing again and again I'd attract the same results. So being a businessperson, I looked at finding my Mr. Right like finding a perfect business to acquire. I removed the emotional aspect of looking for my perfect mate and proceeded from that mindset.

Swipe for Mr. Right

If you're not a business minded person, look at finding Mr. Right as a game. Many of my clients enjoyed this aspect of the process because they have told me, especially women, that they allow themselves to get hurt when their emotions get in the way. That is why we refer to the kids' game Stop Light as a fun way to stay focused without stressing out.

Most people used to call online dating the necessary evil to finding love. I explain that you don't have to go online at all. I just find it an effective way to get the looking process kicked into high gear. In fact, I've shared with every client that preparing for going online forces the average person to self evaluate who they are so they can outline who is right for them. We help you go deeper into that process for yourself so you become very sure who is perfect for you. No more guesswork. No more attracting Mr. Wrong. It's all about knowing your perfect match and keeping focused on the prize.

Bottom line, whether you find someone online or in the real world, it's just as important either way to know who you are and who matches perfectly with you.

For more FREE information, Dating Hints & Tips, Profile Building Templates, Go To:
www.moreloveforyou.com

The Allure of Finding Mr. Right on Online Dating Websites

CHAPTER 2
Knowing Yourself

"The most painful thing is losing yourself
in the process of loving someone too much
and forgetting that you are special too."

— Ernest Hemingway, Men Without Women

- ❤ Why is it important to know yourself before selecting your Mr. Right?
- ❤ Why is it important to come from a place of authenticity instead of need and desperation?
- ❤ With online dating, why do you need to be even more prepared than regular dating?

- Can online dating be overwhelming or frightening?
- How do you set the right intention?
- How do you stay connected and grounded to who you are?

Why is it important to know yourself before selecting your Mr. Right?

> "Open your arms to change, but
> don't let go of your values."
>
> —The Dalai Lama XIV.

In relation to online dating, it means you shouldn't lose yourself in someone else's values, beliefs, hobbies, or interests just to be in a relationship.

- Loving yourself is crucial to choosing the right mate. Instead of changing yourself to fit into their life, you both need to fit into each other's life like perfect pieces of a puzzle.
- Understanding your own values, goals, and desires is the foundation for selecting a compatible partner. When you know who you are and what you want, you can better recognize the qualities and values that align with your own.
- Self-awareness empowers you to set clear boundaries in a relationship. It ensures you will not compromise on essential aspects that define your well-being, such as respect, communication, and personal space.

Knowing Yourself

- ❤ Knowing yourself allows you to assess your compatibility with potential partners more accurately. It helps you identify common interests and values, reducing the chances of entering a relationship where fundamental incompatibilities exist.

- ❤ Selecting Mr. Right is not just about finding the perfect match but also about fostering personal growth. A partner who complements your qualities and supports your growth can be a source of inspiration and motivation.

- ❤ Self-awareness enhances communication skills. When you understand your own communication style and needs, it becomes easier to express yourself clearly and understand your partner's perspectives, leading to healthier interactions.

A client I'll call Sharon set a deadline that she'd be married and on her way to buying a new house by Christmas. Unfortunately, she put a great deal pressure on herself (and others) by forcing a result that should happen organically.

Though the men Sharon dated initially liked her, she made them feel uncomfortable by being aggressive and overtly assertive.

"One man said he liked me a lot, and that he could imagine having children with me," Sharon told me. "But he couldn't imagine living with me because of my overbearing behavior."

I thought it was odd for someone to say that to a potential mate. He loved the way she looked. He liked her homemaking skills and her business savvy. But he didn't like her forcing things to happen as they were just getting to know each other.

"You want to marry the person you want to be with for the rest of your life. The future father of your children. Your best friend forever," I told her.

Sharon had become so focused on crossing things off her checklist that she didn't check in with her inner child to know who she really was.

Apparently, men were initially attracted to her because of her exotic appearance, but lost interest because her negative vibration, and her contrived and unnatural behavior.

Because she'd set her expectations too high, she repelled potential suitors instead of drawing them closer.

Knowing yourself includes recognizing your emotional strengths and vulnerabilities. This self-awareness equips you to navigate the ups and downs of a relationship with greater resilience and understanding. Sharon did not know herself well enough at that time to understand how she was pushing away her potential Mr. Right by trying to make him fit within her schedule of key life completions like he as an item on a shopping list.

People who are unfamiliar with their own emotional triggers and past relationship patterns may unknowingly repeat unhealthy behaviors. Knowing yourself allows you to identify and break these cycles. If Sharon was in tune with who she really was instead of what she wanted, she would not repel possible suitors. Her ego of wanting her ideal life partner overwhelmed her truly loving nature. Her potential love prospect sensed that disconnect. Her ego-based behavior was detrimental to her intentions of attracting her Mr. Right.

Ultimately, by knowing yourself, you're better equipped to find a partner who aligns with your values and supports your journey to a happy and fulfilling life together.

Why is it important to come from a place of authenticity instead of need and desperation?

First, people tend to repeat the same behavior and relationships. Many of my clients say, "All the good people are taken, and there's nobody left." That's not true because the world contains millions of people.

Second, your authenticity is the net you'll cast into the gigantic ocean of single people. Creating a profile containing your hobbies, interests, what you're made of, what motivates and inspires you, and what fires you up to get you up in the morning will be the bait to help you catch the right fish.

There's no net if you don't create a foundation of authenticity before you go online. Your profile containing innocuous things like you like jazz, boating, yachting, skiing, and playing golf will be a shallow attempt at describing who you really are.

Third, list ten (or more) of your top values and beliefs so that your profile contains the essence of who you truly are. Creating a plan of action before you write it will help attract the right person through your vibration and frequency.

Fearful of not being enough (attractive enough, intelligent enough, young enough, etc.), people often embellish their profile to get dates (which, to be honest, is lying). They waste their date's time getting ready for the date, driving to a predesignated location, only to be disappointed because their date was not what they expected. Because that profile builds a false personality, the cycle repeats. They become frustrated and disgusted, and think online dating is for the birds.

Posting an online profile without first creating a foundation of authenticity is like throwing pasta to the ceiling to see what sticks. You'll end up with a huge sticky mess to clean up afterward.

It's imperative to prepare yourself for online dating because of the speed and intensity of being in front of people you wouldn't normally find in a normal dating situation.

Knowing Yourself

Let's say you don't know how to use a computer, or you don't know how to go online, or you just don't like the idea of meeting somebody through a sterile medium like the Internet. Instead, you decide to go to church and tell everybody that you're single and available.

Being in a room full of strangers can feel very disconcerting as you're all flying blind. You go to singles events where you meet a few duds. You go to a networking mixer and meet more duds. People invite you to dinner because they think they have the perfect person for you, but they turn out to be another dud.

Repeatedly meeting people that don't resonate with you can be frustrating. People say, "I hate being single," or "I hate the dating scene" because they're not clear about what they want.

However, it's a fallacy to say there's a dating scene as it's purely from your perspective. If nothing is written down or clearly visualized, you can't manifest the proper traits in a person you want to date. It's like being in war, which dating is often considered. You're shell-shocked because of dismally failed relationships or dating experiences, which puts up a wall that prevents you from meeting potential partners.

With online dating, why do you need to be even more prepared than regular dating?

No matter where you live, you can randomly meet people at a car wash, a restaurant, or at a grocery store. But chances are, like the earlier bowl of pasta, nothing will stick as you don't have common interests, goals, priorities, values, and beliefs.

As the years fly by, you remain single, sad, miserable, and frustrated because you're meeting people one at a time, which is a waste of your valuable time. Whereas if you go online, and create the correct profile, you can sort through hundreds of people to find just the right one.

Can online dating be overwhelming or frightening?

Maybe. But it doesn't have to be daunting if you create the right mindset before you go online.

Did I go out with all 2,874 guys who contacted me while I was searching for the right partner? No! I gently emailed the others by saying, "I'm so sorry – we are not a right match. But God bless you... I hope you find the love of your life." Then I deleted their profile from my inbox to prevent further contact.

The 87 men I went out with were quality men (I wished I had a lot of single girlfriends I could refer them to, but alas, that didn't happen). I attracted wonderful men because of my positive vibration and frequency. I read my affirmations and manifestation list that contained traits I wanted in a future husband, not just a boyfriend, which was important to clarify.

Knowing Yourself

Going online with the right profile magnetizes you to attract eligible, fantastic men who will love and respect you because they have the same frequency, vibration, core characteristics and as a bonus, hobbies, and interests.

My husband Jim and I share many key core characteristics. In fact, we share four out of our top five core values. We shared a few hobbies and interests, but there were many that we didn't share. I love tennis, he loves basketball. I love downhill skiing and he would rather throw snowballs in the winter. Some of the nine men that I was previously engaged to played tennis or loved to ski as well, but we didn't share four out of five top core values. I don't think that I was even aware of my top five values. Maybe I was unconsciously, which is why when I got closer to those previous marriage dates, a voice inside me said, "Run and don't look back!", which I did. I knew that even though those previously engaged men were fine first class marriage material, they were not for me.

By the way, as Jim and I got to know each other, we began to create our own shared hobbies and interests. I introduced Jim to Smooth Jazz, which we enjoy together. In turn, I've grown to appreciate his Rock and Roll classics. And just recently, I discovered Bluegrass music. Who would figure a girl from Beverly Hills would toe-tap to Bluegrass by the side of the Tennessee River?

Knowing your own personal traits that guide your life is crucial to knowing who your Mr. Right should be. Once you whittle down potential partners who seem to have the right traits, you'll further hone the process of elimination with five top questions (which is in another chapter).

How do you set the right intention?

Many negative distractions can pull you away from who you truly are (i.e., TV commercials, billboards, Internet websites, social media, political and violent news reports, YouTube, etc.), so you need to be firm about your intention for dating online.

For example, is your intention to build your ego by getting a lot of attention? Or is it to genuinely find someone to spend your life with?

My client, Margaret, was married for 30 years when her husband passed away.

"Dr. Renée, I'd love to take your workshop and work with you," she said hesitantly. "But I don't want to do that right now as I'm a newly singled widow. I want to check online dating out first to see what it's all about."

She went online and dated several men, and one very kind, generous man fell madly in love with her. Six months into their relationship her daughter had Margaret's first grandchild. She spent a lot of time doting on the child while unintentionally ignoring the boyfriend, who at first was okay with it because he understood the circumstances.

After about a year of dating, Margaret shared the changes in their relationship.

"When your daughter became pregnant," I reminded her, "I mentioned the possibility he wouldn't like it for these very reasons."

"I'm so upset," Margaret continued. "I don't know how to break up with him. He's been so kind and generous and has given me so many beautiful gifts. But I'm not in love with him anymore. The sad thing is I know we could have made it."

"Yes, you definitely could have," I said. "But because you didn't go deep within yourself to find out what you really wanted, you wasted your time and his time. You broke his heart, which I know you feel very bad about. The downside is you get to see your grandchild. But then you come home to an empty bed, which is a terrible feeling."

Dating is a package deal as it includes your families, friends, inner circles, and pets who existed before this person came into your life. Therefore, I tell my clients that setting correct intentions for a relationship can prevent the empty bed syndrome.

Before you enter a relationship, ask yourself these questions and more.

- Will this person accept my family?
- Will they accept a new grandchild (depending on your age)?
- Will they accept a pet (dog, cat, hamster, etc.)?
- Will they accept my friends?
- Will they accept my love of (fill in the blank of a hobby, sport, or passion that will consume time that you may not now have together)?

"Margaret," I said, "you want someone to stand by you during good and bad times. A brand-new grandchild is a big deal. But someone who can't relate to children or already has had children and grandchildren can become jealous of the time you spend with them. Therefore, going forward, setting the right intentions with your values and beliefs will attract the right person into your life."

Margaret became my client, and with her new understanding of intention, she went on a search for her true love, which she found in short order.

How do you stay connected and grounded to who you are?

The best way to stay connected is to state your affirmations with intention.

My top values are Love, God, Spirituality, Family, Finance, and Legacy, but for now I'll discuss spirituality. Everyone has different beliefs and values, and this is purely what I'm sharing about myself.

Two powerful words I share with my clients are "I am" as they're a part of God, who's in all of us. I am a child of God. I am favored by God. I believe in God. God helps me throughout my day. You can even say things like "I am powerful" and "I am unlimited."

You want to repeat affirmations while standing in front of a mirror, or wherever you are, to establish them in your subconscious mind. (You can print them out, then put them in a plastic photo sleeve, or laminate them to keep them handy.)

You don't need materialism to make you happy. Being authentic to who you are and what you want creates happiness in whatever environment you're in.

Summary

Knowing yourself is imperative before you begin looking for your soulmate. Who you are is not the job you perform or the hobbies and sports you spend your time on. It's much deeper than that.

A value is characteristic of who you are. It is non-negotiable. Most people have seven to ten values that they focus on. Values are the lenses through which we see life and make decisions. They are formed at a very early age and follow us throughout our lives.

Beliefs also direct our actions in life, but they are not as concrete as values. A belief is a function of experience, and if an experience changes or the information that contributes to an experience changes, the belief can adjust or change completely.

Hobbies and interests may be influenced by our values and beliefs, but they are not the core of who we are. Many people base their relationships on hobbies and interests more than on what they truly believe in. They may get along as a couple at first, but their individual values and beliefs will rule the direction of their relationship and their decision-making, so they need to be compatible. Know yourself first.

Homework:

Give yourself the gift of discovering your top seven or eight values. Read the following twenty questions to help you get into an introspective mood. Take a clean sheet of paper, or better yet, get yourself a notebook or journal devoted to the work you are now doing for yourself, and a blue-ink pen (make sure it's blue—I'll explain why later)—and answer the questions to the best of your ability. Once you have completed that part (don't forget the bonus question below the twenty questions), write what you think and feel are your top values. Remember, they must be items that are a must in your life and non-negotiable. Don't worry about the order at first; just get them down on paper. If you have more than seven or eight values, that's okay, but be aware that the top seven or eight values will impact you the most in a long-term relationship.

Once have your set of top values, put them in order of importance. Take your time on this process. Your values hierarchy is almost as important as the values themselves, so take your time and enjoy the process.

Remember, this is the foundation of everything else you're going to do from here on out, so don't rush to get to the fun part of the exercise that outlines what you're looking for because without this foundation, nothing you build will last or stand strong. In fact, if you didn't complete the rest of this book, you will have more success by doing this exercise than from anything else you learn in this book. That's how important it is to know yourself first.

Why write your values down if you unconsciously know them?

Our values direct us in times of need. The importance of consciously knowing them is that they become identified awareness. The merging of the conscious and unconscious is very powerful and makes a huge difference when attracting your Mr. Right.

Remember those times that attracted your Mr. Wrong and after that awful inevitable breakup you swore that you'd never, ever do that again…then you do it again? If you allowed your conscious and unconscious to assist you in your decision making, it won't happen again. Isn't that reassuring?

Here are some interesting introspective questions that might help you find out who you are, what you value, and what your beliefs are:

- ❤ What is your idea of ultimate happiness?
- ❤ What are you most fearful of?
- ❤ What character trait do you most hate about yourself?
- ❤ What trait do you hate most in others?
- ❤ Which person, living or deceased, do you most admire?
- ❤ What is your greatest extravagance?
- ❤ What do you consider the most over-rated virtue?
- ❤ What do you dislike about your appearance?
- ❤ What is the quality you most like in a man or woman?
- ❤ Who or what is the greatest love of your life?
- ❤ Where and when are you happiest?
- ❤ If you could change one thing about yourself, what would it be?
- ❤ What do you consider your greatest achievement?
- ❤ Where would you most like to live?
- ❤ What is your most treasured possession?
- ❤ What do you most value in your friends?
- ❤ What is it that you most dislike?

- ❤ What is your greatest regret?
- ❤ How would you like to die?
- ❤ What is your motto?

"What I know about myself for sure is _____."

To help you determine what your top seven or eight values may be, review the following list of values and circle the ten values that speak to you. List them on a separate piece of paper. Then put them in hierarchal order of importance from one to ten and keep that list. Write down your top seven or eight values in your notebook or journal.

List of Values

A-D	E-M	O-Z
Abundance	Eagerness	Obedience
Acceptance	Economy	Open-Mindedness
Accomplishment	Ecstasy	Openness
Achievement	Education	Optimism
Acknowledgment	Effectiveness	Order
Activeness	Elegance	Originality
Adaptability	Empathy	Outrageousness
Adoration	Encouragement	Passion

A-D	E-M	O-Z
Adventure	Endurance	Peace
Affection	Energy	Perfection
Affluence	Enjoyment	Perseverance
Aggressiveness	Entertainment	Persistence
Altruism	Enthusiasm	Persuasiveness
Ambition	Excellence	Philanthropy
Appreciation	Excitement	Playfulness
Approachability	Expertise	Pleasure
Assertiveness	Exploration	Power
Attractiveness	Expressiveness	Practicality
Balance	Extravagance	Preparedness
Beauty	Exuberance	Proactivity
Being the Best	Fairness	Professionalism
Bliss	Faith	Prosperity
Boldness	Fame	Realism
Bravery	Family	Reliability
Brilliance	Fashion	Religiousness
Calmness	Fearlessness	Resilience
Candor	Fierceness	Resourcefulness
Care	Financial Independence	Respect
Carefulness	Fitness	Sacrifice
Certainty	Flexibility	Security

Knowing Yourself

A-D	E-M	O-Z
Challenge	Focus	Self-Control
Charity	Fortitude	Selflessness
Chastity	Frankness	Self-Reliance
Cheerfulness	Freedom	Sensitivity
Clarity	Friendliness	Sensuality
Cleanliness	Frugality	Serenity
Clear-Mindedness	Fun	Service
Cleverness	Generosity	Sexuality
Comfort	Giving	Significance
Commitment	Grace	Sincerity
Compassion	Gratitude	Skillfulness
Connection	Gregariousness	Sophistication
Consistency	Growth	Spirit
Contribution	Happiness	Spirituality
Control	Harmony	Strength
Cooperation	Health	Success
Courage	Helpfulness	Sympathy
Courtesy	Heroism	Synergy
Creativity	Holiness	Teamwork
Credibility	Honesty	Thoroughness
Cunning	Honor	Thrift
Curiosity	Hopefulness	Tidiness

A-D	E-M	O-Z
Daring	Hospitality	Timeliness
Decisiveness	Humility	Traditionalism
Dependability	Humor	Trustworthiness
Determination	Independence	Truth
Devoutness	Integrity	Understanding
Dignity	Intelligence	Unflappability
Diligence	Joy	Uniqueness
Directness	Knowledge	Victory
Discipline	Leadership	Vitality
Discovery	Liberty	Wealth
Dominance	Love	Winning
Duty	Loyalty	Wisdom
Dynamism	Making a Difference	Youthfulness

For more FREE information, Dating Hints & Tips, Profile Building Templates, Go To:
www.moreloveforyou.com

Knowing Yourself

CHAPTER THREE
Knowing What You Want

"Insanity: doing the same thing over and over again and expecting different results."

— Albert Einstein

- What's the number one mistake that could derail your online dating efforts?
- Do you have an example of how to prevent attracting the wrong life partner?
- Are you saying that you need to write down exactly what you want in a partner?

- Should you focus on your perfect partner's core characteristics first or their favorite activities and hobbies?
- Do you have an example of clients whose values and beliefs matched, but their hobbies and activities didn't necessarily match?
- You often hear that opposites attract. Is that because they look like opposites on the surface when it's deeper than that?
- What's the best tactic for someone to attract their perfect partner?
- What's exactly is a manifestation decree?
- Why does this attraction process work?
- How does energetic vibration work when you say the statement every day?
- Does repeating your manifestation decree while being in that kinetic frequency emit a signal of like attracts like?
- Can you tell us why being a chameleon, as opposed to being authentic, can be hurtful to your chances of finding the perfect mate?
- Explain further how I attract my Mr. Right?

What's the number one mistake that could derail your online dating efforts?

Before you leap into online dating, know that you'll repeat the same behavior and mistakes if you haven't worked on yourself. If you've had one or more online relationships, or you just broke up with someone, you need to first write down what you want in an ideal mate (what I call a "manifestation decree"), then create a profile that matches your vision.

It shouldn't be about what they do for a living, their hobbies, what kind of car they drive, etc. Basing it on your values and beliefs will manifest the loving partner you deserve. Your core characteristics are the foundation of a life-long, loving partnership. As we shared with you in the previous chapters, hobbies and interests are secondary in your search or like I would say, "It's the cherry on top of the sundae." The ice cream, sauce, whipped cream, and nuts make up the most important part of the sundae just like your core characteristics make up the essence of who you really are in life. Your Mr. Right doesn't have to be a downhill skier if that's an interest and sport you enjoy. However, they should share similar top core characteristics as you do to support a loving life together.

Swipe for Mr. Right
Do you have an example of how to prevent attracting the wrong life partner?

Preventing the attraction of the wrong life partner is a crucial step in building a healthy and fulfilling relationship. Establishing and maintaining clear boundaries is a powerful example of how to achieve this. I can't stress enough that you need to acknowledge your core characteristics on your dating profile. For example, some people faithfully go to church every Sunday or practice their own form of spirituality. Since church and spirituality are two different distinctions, you will need to clarify what you want in a mate. For example, if you are, and they need to be, a devout Christian, Catholic, Muslim, Jew, or agnostic, then you need to present clearly that this is important to you. Too many people are attracted by outward appearance, which many people refer to as chemistry, and use this attraction to make their choice of a life partner. Choices need to be made primarily from the core foundation of who you are.

If you're more spiritual and free-spirited and believe that God is the Universal Father and the true source of love, you might want to include that to attract a like-minded mate. If you believe in Agape love, or you have a sanctuary in your home where you pray or meditate, you might want to include that you're a devout spiritualist and believe in a higher being.

My second most important value is family. If you're like me, you need to include in your profile that you spend time on the weekends with your family and your children, and you see your parents on a regular basis. This lets people know they'll need to have the same values to be part of your life, or at the very least, they need to be okay with you spending every other weekend with your family and offspring.

Even though you have not yet met your ideal mate, by firmly stating your wants and desires you will attract only those people who share your ideals of a perfect life. Why waste your time, money and attention on a person who doesn't match your ideal life partner when that perfect Mr. Right is waiting patiently for you. But don't wait too long.

Through these examples, we see that prevention starts with a deep understanding of one's own needs and the courage to communicate and uphold boundaries. By doing so, you prevent attracting the wrong life partner and create space for a healthier, more compatible relationship to enter your life. These examples illustrate the power of boundaries in shaping the dynamics of romantic relationships and guiding you away from incompatible partners.

Are you saying that you need to write down exactly what you want in a partner?

Yes. It's just like writing a business plan where you have a beginning, middle and an end. Instead, this is the personal business of manifesting the man or woman of your dreams. Creating a plan prevents surprises and assures certainty for everlasting love. And isn't that the whole point of falling in love?

My clients often ask how many people I have in my database? Do you have any blondes (or whatever the case may be)? I want to go out with this one… or this one… Let me be clear: I'm not a matchmaker. I don't hook people up for dates or find somebody to go with them to a black-tie event, a family affair, or a holiday party. My process provides the steps to get you ready to sign up for online dating, or to meet someone at a grocery store, at church, or at a synagogue.

Writing your values and beliefs down on paper, then adding the kind of person you want to grow old with, is a deeper, more succinct way of finding your true love. I know it seems simple. But it's not easy. The growing trend has been total convenience in everything we do. Have a headache, pop a pill. Need to lose weight, pop another pill. Hungry, call Uber Eats and pay $30+ for a burger, fries, and soft drink. When holidays are around the corner, you don't want to go through the humiliation of explaining why you are again alone to your family and/or work friends. So maybe if you go online and pick someone cute, and blah, blah, blah story. Don't do what everyone else does and just get whatever photo of yourself that may be still in this same decade and jot down just enough interesting facts about who you are and who would be a good match for you. Don't fall for that convenient game again. After all, "How is that been working for you so far?"

If you have a headache, drink some water. You may be dehydrated. If you need to lose weight, cut your portions and go out for a walk. If you're hungry, plan a meal and cook it at home. And if you're going to look for your Mr. Right, plan the time to learn about your core characteristics and base your search online on what you desire in a life mate. This is an investment of time that will pay off exponentially for your love life.

Should you focus on your perfect partner's core characteristics first or their favorite activities and hobbies?

Like I said earlier, it's more important to focus on your manifestation decree that states exactly who you want. Are they family-oriented? Are they spiritual? What kind of work do they do?

Do they have an employee mindset or do they have an entrepreneur mindset? This is important to clarify because these are two completely different mindsets. One is higher risk with a higher payoff, whereas the other is lower risk with a lower payoff. For example, an employee mindset is clocking in at eight o'clock in the morning, then clocking out at five o'clock. There's low-risk certainty in getting a monthly paycheck.

My husband's first wife, a very lovely lady who I greatly enjoy visiting when we come to town, has a defiantly employee mindset. She has done very well in her career and craves the financial security a traditional job provides. On the other hand, my husband is a definite entrepreneur at heart but is flexible enough to play the role of an employee. When my husband had a world-class restaurant years before he became a speaker, author, and trainer, his wife couldn't understand why he could not be home sooner in the evenings. She knew that the restaurant closed at 10:00 pm but at the earliest, he would be home at 11:30 pm. As an entrepreneur, he knew the value of going from table to table thanking his patrons for coming to his restaurant that evening while his employees headed home. Could they have gotten over this difference? Possibly. All I know is that they are both happier now because he can be unapologetically his full self and she the same. They are with life partners who always support who they are. You should have that for yourself as well.

Characteristics like honoring their children and their family, being respectful to their co-workers and people in general are in the deep end of the pool that contains values and core characteristics that keep a relationship going forever and create your everlasting love. Whereas things like favorite activities or hobbies, working out, going to the gym, driving exotic cars, going to concerts, traveling, and more, are in the shallow end of the pool. There is nothing wrong with those activities and hobbies. Just don't base your decision making on characteristics that come and go. Build your relationship foundation on solid, real-world values and beliefs and you'll benefit greatly in life.

Do you have an example of clients whose values and beliefs matched, but their hobbies and activities didn't necessarily match?

A client said that he and his wife got divorced after twenty-five years of marriage because they just couldn't get along. His priority was his family and his boys, and being a nine-to-five employee, whereas her priority was having a prominent role in an entertainment company and sitting on the board of directors. They also had contrasting hobbies, so they broke up because they didn't have anything in common.

After their divorce, he still enjoyed hobbies like wine-tasting and spending time with his boys. Then he met a woman who also had strong family values and a belief in God. Besides being of the same faith, and having strong family values, they had many other things in common such as their employee mindsets.

She's not as much into wine or food as he is, but their strong family values are parallel to each other. Coming home at night at a certain time and having dinner on the table is in the shallow end of their love pool. Their engrained beliefs and values are in the deep end of the pool, so they perfectly balance each other. Their marriage works because their hobbies and activities might differ, but their values and beliefs are the same. By the way, they're still happily married, and have a child whom they named Renée!

You often hear that opposites attract. Is that because they look like opposites on the surface when it's deeper than that?

On the surface it might look like people are yin and yang, and a perfect match. But the values they hold dear to their hearts must be in sync. For example, the couple I previously mentioned are best friends, which to me is the secret of a lasting relationship. Having a fantastic, enduring relationship isn't just about love, but also about values, beliefs, acknowledgement, attention, affection, and respect.

The opposites that most people notice are their respective interests or like I point out, if you're in a heterosexual relationship, men and women are opposites naturally. Yes, is this a generality in characteristics. Of course, it is, but it's fun to notice those differences.

An example that Jim likes to point out is that I regularly tell him that I can get ready to go out at a moments notice. Jim adds to that belief statement with, "…compared to other women". When it's early morning workout time, he'll jump out of bed and run down to the gym before I wipe the sleep out of my eyes. Our differences continue. He is a minimalist while I enjoy a variety of life's gifts around me. In business, he can be very focused and sometimes can be perceived as being cold while I still have a very hospitable connection with people around me. We are different, but we are always connected. It's a beautiful way to live to allow your significant other to personify their bliss in life while allowing you to do the same. Because of our own personal foundation of values, all other interests and hobbies are secondary in our lives.

What's the best tactic for someone to attract their perfect partner?

The best tactic is to write down exactly what you want. I know I've shared a great deal about values and beliefs when I refer to your core characteristics, but you might include things that are deal-breakers too.

While creating my manifestation decree, I emphasized meeting someone who had a strong spiritual belief. Belonging to an organized church wasn't as important as was believing in God. Regarding their spirituality, I wanted someone between at least a nine or a ten (ten being the highest), so an atheist or an agnostic was definitely not in my realm of possibilities. This needed to be written down in my manifestation decree.

I wanted someone who gave me the freedom to do what I wanted whenever I wanted to do it. I didn't want to attract someone who'd suffocate me. Instead, I wanted someone who'd give me the freedom to express who I am as a woman and an entrepreneur. Since I'm a very strong woman, and have strong opinions, they needed to be secure enough in themselves to support me in my decisions and not always challenge everything I'd say or do.

Besides believing in God, and not smoking (cigars occasionally were okay, but never cigarettes), I wanted them to take at least one or two showers a day, so they didn't smell bad. That might be trivial to other people. But I have a sensitive sniffer, so I'm a real stickler for proper hygiene.

I also wanted somebody who didn't tear up the bed during the night, as that would mean I'd lose sleep by having to constantly struggle with the sheets and blankets. Again, that's kind of a small thing, but it was in my top ten on my manifestation decree.

I wanted them to love my pets. I had a little dog at the time, and lots of birds and fish. For some people it's just not their thing, but that was important to me. Though these requests are in the shallow part of a relationship, not having these compatible assets can be red flags and deal-breakers.

You need to know your own dealbreakers. We have a document that lists various activities that have a check-off box that gives you a choice between, Must, Maybe and Never. If you don't want to have a cigarette smoker in your home, you should check off "Never" in your list. The reason that I can accept a cigar smoker is that cigar smokers typically light up infrequently compared to cigarette smokers. Remember, you have to live with this person and these habits compounded over years together add up. So be clear, knowing your Musts, Maybes and Nevers are vital.

What's exactly is a manifestation decree?

A manifestation decree is a letter of any length that you write to the Universe about your dreams and desires. My manifestation decree was fifty-seven pages, which seems long. But since I wanted to be very specific about what I did and didn't want, I put it in the context of everything I wanted. Remember, this is for attracting your life partner. The time that you invest in writing a manifestation decree is worth every second put into it. Most of my clients groan and complain about taking the time to write this letter or decree until I remind them that most people put more effort into their vacation planning than planning for their ideal life partner. Maybe it's time to change?

Once you write down your partner's attributes, you'll speak and read your affirmations and manifestations in the present tense. You won't say this "is going to happen" or "I did find this, now I have to find this." Instead, you say, "The person I wrote down on paper is coming into my awareness" because the Universe needs clarity to know who to send you.

No matter whether your manifestation decree is one or thirty pages long, write everything in the present tense. "My everlasting love adores [not will love] my children and my pets as much as I love them." Or "My life partner accepts me for who I am" instead of "will accept me." Therefore, writing in present tense assures that it will happen now and not in some unknown timeframe.

Instead of saying, "I want someone who doesn't take a shower every day," I said, "The love of my life must take one to two showers per day." Never use the words "doesn't" or "not" as they're too ambiguous for the Universe to understand. If you're in your car, when you wake up in the morning, or before you go to bed, you'll firmly state "I have attracted…" or "I have in my life the perfect man (or woman) of my dreams" or "the man (or woman) of my manifestations."

No matter how long your manifestation decree is, you can keep adding to it as you think of things you want in an ideal mate. But always remember to say it in present tense, such as, "I am grateful that I have found my true love, the man (or woman) of my dreams in my manifestation decree."

Why does this attraction process work?

It works because it's whatever you believe you want, which is why it's so important to be specific about your lifestyle, your environment, and the people you want around you.

It's especially important if you're a single parent, you have pets, or you have a distinctive lifestyle because you don't want to conform to someone else's lifestyle completely; you want someone who's adaptable so you can find a balance between the two lifestyles.

You want someone who makes your life less stressful, who's your true complement, and who accepts you for who you are and vice versa. You shouldn't try to change them, nor should they try to change you. You both need to accept each other without judgment or criticism. If you haven't experienced this in a life partner yet, then it's hard for you to visualize this for yourself. Does this reduce your pool of possibilities? Yes, it very well will shrink what you consider marrying material. But who cares. You're only looking for the "one." When I first set up my dating website, I was overwhelmed by the vast number of responses. It wasn't until I tightened up my manifestation decree (this is only for me, not for sharing) that I tightened up my profile description to reflect who I was looking for, did the number of responses become somewhat manageable over a reasonable time frame. This is exactly how you use your own profile. Don't look at this as a popularity contest. The more volume you attract, the more overwhelmed you'll become. Be true to what you desire and attract the one, not the many.

How does energetic vibration work when you say the statement on a daily basis?

Thoughts create words. Words spoken or read create vibrations. Vibration spreads throughout the universe. Your thoughts about your Mr. Right that you write into your manifestation decree create energy that vibrates at a certain frequency. Saying your manifestation decree out-loud creates a vibration into the Universe that can penetrate through cement, metal, or lead. For example, stating, "I have found the love of my life" in Los Angeles will attract someone in New York or anywhere in the world because your kinetic vibration is so powerful. As much as this sounds "woo-woo" or new age beliefs, science is constantly proving this idea is real and what you manifest from your thoughts and words reaches the person for whom it was intended.

The concept of attracting like energy in the universe is rooted in fundamental principles of science. At its core, this idea aligns with the law of attraction, which suggests that positive or negative thoughts and energies can influence one's experiences and outcomes. Quantum physics provides a scientific framework to explain this phenomenon, as it demonstrates that the energy and vibrations we emit can impact the quantum field around us. When we radiate positive energy and thoughts, we may resonate with similar frequencies in the universe, potentially leading to more positive experiences and interactions. In essence, the science of attraction underscores the interconnectedness of energy, thoughts, and the outcomes we manifest in our lives.

Have you ever experienced a time when you arbitrarily thought of a friend who you hadn't talked to for a while then within minutes you get a phone call from that person? You just experienced the results of the law of attraction.

Does repeating your manifestation decree while being in that kinetic frequency emit a signal of like attracts like?

The saying "be careful what you wish for" is absolutely true. Like does attract like, which is why being specific about what you want, and knowing yourself, is key to living your dream life.

The first step in my process is to know who you are. Many of my clients have been chameleons throughout their entire lives by adapting to other people's personalities, views, and lifestyle. However, they long to be the best version of themselves by being authentic to who they truly are. They want to be accepted and loved for who they are, instead of being judged by people who want them to be something they aren't.

Many people don't realize that they are living a coward's life by not being who they truly are. This is why I was confused when I was in those nine wonderful potential husbands that I broke it off with just before our wedding. I enjoyed the time together with them. It was like I was always visiting. Like the hen, I was interested in contributing to the breakfast with eggs, unlike the pig who was committed. Maybe not the best metaphor, but you get it. I was always a visitor in these men's lives. There was no room for me because their life was already full. But I took responsibility for living a chameleon life and by failed engagement #9, I began to point my finger in the mirror as to why I was where I was in my not married life.

Can you tell us why being a chameleon, as opposed to being authentic, can be hurtful to your chances of finding the perfect mate?

Being a chameleon 24/7 is like being in your own prison. You'll be miserable because you can't keep pretending. Life isn't about being on stage and pretending; it's about being authentic and true to who you are.

If you stay stuck in a prison you mentally built for yourself, you'll resent the person you're with, which will create friction and resentment. They won't know where your anger is coming from because you're not being authentic to who you really are. Don't waste your life on being a chameleon. Be authentic to who you really are. If you haven't made time to list your top life values, do it now. Don't wait. Get clear on who you are so you can now design your Mr. Right sooner than later.

Explain further how I attract my Mr. Right.

Your attraction letter or as I call it, your manifestation decree, is the visionary tool that will get you on the right track immediately. Next, I'll share another understanding of how you broadcast and receive specific information naturally through a process call the Reticular Activating System.

Knowing What You Want

The Reticular Activating System (RAS) is a crucial neurological network within the brainstem that acts as a filter for the vast amount of sensory information we encounter daily. It works by selectively focusing our attention on what's deemed important based on our goals and priorities. Think of it as a personalized search engine for your brain. When we set specific objectives or pay attention to particular details, the RAS helps us notice relevant information while filtering out the rest. This mechanism plays a pivotal role in our daily lives, from recognizing a familiar face in a crowded room to honing our focus on achieving our goals or in this case, recognizing your Mr. Right when you see, hear, or sense him. This is why it's so important to be thorough in your manifestation decree. Start somewhere and begin. I suggest that you use the questionnaire below to help you joggle your mind to see what is important to you in a life partner. Take your time and enjoy the process. Sometimes if I get stuck, I ask the question, "Who is the perfect person for me and what are their important characteristics," just before I doze off to sleep. When you wake up, be ready with a pen and pad by your nightstand and begin writing before you fully awake. That time between fully asleep and fully awake is a highly creative time to use in this manner.

Action Steps: Manifestation Letter

In a new notebook or journal, begin writing in blue ink your manifestation letter. To get started, use your list and information from Chapter 2: Knowing Yourself as a guideline to get things rolling. Focus first on your ideal mate's values and beliefs. Then organize the rest of the manifestation letter in any way you'd like. Remember to write in the present tense as if it has already happened. If you're not one to sit down and write, make it fun while writing. Play your favorite music in the background or start with the easy stuff first, like what kinds of vacations you'd both like to experience, which places you'd like to see, which concerts you'd like to hear. Remember to include in your descriptions and details as much sensory information as possible like what you see, hear, feel, smell, and taste. This is the most important part of the attracting process after "Knowing Yourself." Take your time and enjoy the process. Does this seem like a lot of work? Yes, it is! But I promise you that if you follow the steps exactly as I have outlined for you, your rewards will outweigh your efforts ten-fold! So be patient; let the power of RAS and your manifestation letter do the heavy lifting. I've included some questions below to stimulate your creative self in this process of Love by Design™. Enjoy!

Bonus Step: "End of the Movie"

(This is for all of those "go-getters" out there committed to finding their Mr. or Mrs. Right quickly.)

Create an "end of the movie" scenario about you and the love of your life. This is a slice of life from the life you've created, starring you and your ideal mate. You can

Knowing What You Want

write this short story on note cards that you carry around with you and read during breaks at the office, during commercials on TV, or while waiting for a call. Put down your iPad or cell phone, stop playing Angry Birds, and enjoy a piece of life. Remember, write everything in the present tense, like "my sweetheart and I are…" not "my sweetheart and I will…." Include in your scenario the following details:

It's Sunday morning and you and your ideal mate are having a leisurely breakfast together. Describe your experience. What aromas do you smell? What do you see? What sounds in the background do you hear? What flavors do you taste? What looks do you get from your lover? What words does he/she say? Remember, you are the star, director, and audience of your "end of the movie" story.

_____
_____
_____
_____
_____
_____
_____
_____
_____
_____
_____
_____
_____

Swipe for Mr. Right

_____
_____
_____

Love by Design™ Questions to Help Fuel Your Creativity in Writing Your Manifestation Decree Letter:

- ❤ What specific values do you cherish that also need to be in your ideal mate's top seven or eight values?

_____
_____
_____
_____
_____
_____
_____
_____
_____
_____

- ❤ What specific beliefs of yours need to be compatible with your ideal mate's beliefs?

_____
_____
_____
_____

Knowing What You Want

_____
_____
_____
_____

❤ Describe what your Mr. or Mrs. Right looks like, sounds like, smells like, and feels like:

_____
_____
_____
_____
_____
_____
_____

❤ What activities or hobbies do you like to do together? What are you okay doing apart?

_____
_____
_____
_____
_____
_____
_____
_____
_____
_____

Swipe for Mr. Right

- ♥ How many showers does your partner need to take as a minimum standard?

_____
_____

- ♥ Does he/she have kids? How old do the kids have to be? Is there a cut-off age, like no babies, but teens are fine?

_____
_____
_____
_____
_____

- ♥ Is he/she clean-shaven or does he/she sport facial hair (both men and women!)?

_____
_____

- ♥ Is your partner physically active? Does he/she play a sport? Are you okay if your partner spends time with that sport?

_____
_____
_____
_____

Knowing What You Want

_____
_____

❤ Is he/she an extrovert or introvert?

_____
_____

❤ Is he/she a dress-up sophisticated type, dress-down casual type, or an appropriate-to-the-occasion kind of person?

_____
_____
_____
_____

❤ Does he/she travel for work? Does he/she work from home?

_____
_____

❤ Is your future partner financially secure? Is money important to him/her?

_____
_____
_____
_____

_____
_____

❤ Does he/she own or rent a home?

_____
_____

❤ Does he/she like to travel?

_____
_____
_____
_____

❤ Is he/she open to personal transformation and development?

_____
_____
_____
_____

Is your future partner religious? Does he/she have to be from a specific religion? Is he/she more spiritual with no ties to a church? Does he/she believe in God?

_____
_____

Knowing What You Want

_____

❤ Does your future partner care for pets? What kinds of pets?

_____

❤ Does he/she get along with his/her parents, siblings, and extended family?

_____

Swipe for Mr. Right

_____
_____
_____
_____
_____
_____

❤ Does he/she have close lifelong friends? Activity friends? Work friends?

_____
_____
_____
_____
_____
_____
_____

❤ Does he/she like to dine out? Dine in? Both? Does he/she cook? Clean up? Both?

_____
_____

- ❤ What kinds of movies does your future partner like? Books? Periodicals? Blogs?

_____
_____
_____
_____

- ❤ Is he/she active in social media? Does he/she use Facebook or tweet?

_____
_____
_____
_____

- ❤ Is he/she a joiner, meaning very social or inclusive?

_____

- ❤ Does he/she belong to clubs, the chamber of commerce, networking groups, etc.?

_____
_____
_____

❤ Is he/she a mountain person, a desert person, a city person, or a coastal person?

❤ What is his/her political affiliation? Does your future partner view him- or herself as more liberal, conservative, or moderate?

❤ Does he/she smoke cigarettes? Cigars? Pipes? E-cigarettes?

Knowing What You Want

- Does he/she meditate, chant, or pray?

- Does he/she enjoy artificially induced altered states (does he/she like to get high!)? How often and for how long?

Make a list of common dating questions like "Does your ideal mate smoke?" and list them in a column. You can use some of the questions that you just read or add the questions that are important to you. Add three more columns titled: Must, Maybe, and Never. Put a check in the column that best answers your questions. For instance, to answer the question about smoking, if you don't care either way whether he or she smokes, check "Maybe." If you checked "Never," then this is what we call a deal breaker and no matter how perfect that person seems to be in other areas, this is the deal breaker, and you need to move on. Remember, this is your life. Don't give in to the short-term thrill of finding a partial love of your life. Go all the way to get the person you deserve by sticking to the long-term plan of finding your love at last!

For more FREE information, Dating Hints & Tips, Profile Building Templates, Go To:
www.moreloveforyou.com

Knowing What You Want

CHAPTER FOUR
Designing Your Profile

> "You are the designer of your destiny;
> you are the author of your story."
>
> —Lisa Nichols

- ❤ Can I get someone else to write my dating profile?
- ❤ What are the five parts of designing your perfect profile?

Swipe for Mr. Right
Can I get someone else to write my dating profile?

Yes, but they will not as authentic as you are when you follow these simple steps yourself.

You now know there's a lot more required to create your search, so you'll understand why I've put this part at the end of the book, not right up front or even in the middle. Finding Mr. or Mrs. Right is all about creating the circumstances to attract that person, not advertise for that person. As I've said before, online searching for your soulmate is a very effective tool. Heck, that's how I found Jim. But you must do the foundational work before you jump into the boiling pot of online dating.

With that said, many of my clients have asked for help in this area. They want to do all the groundwork so they can express themselves clearly by using this powerful search tool. What I tell them is that if you've done your homework from this book already, this part should be simple.

What are the five parts of designing your perfect profile?

1. Headline
2. Headshots and Pictures
3. Who You Are
4. What You Want
5. Contact Information

Let's look at each one in detail:

Headline:

Remember, this is what got my honey to take notice of me. If you're a woman, don't ask someone to be your soulmate. It's way too soon for that. And if he responds that he will, he probably won't last. Do be a bit outrageous. Remember, it's an attention getter. This is also a good time to express who you are without saying who you are.

I used the headline, Ex-Model/Chef, which was also accurate. I was a former Shiseido cosmetics model, and I am also a formally trained and experienced chef. I was being me but stating it in a way that made people curious. Jim liked the duality of the headline. On one hand, a model is focused on looking good all the time, meaning she is always dieting to stay fit and look lean for the camera. On the other hand, while a trained chef will express herself with food and freely taste all her creations, she is unconcerned about the calorie count. This got Jim to check out who this person was and find out whether the headline was accurate.

Have fun with your headline. Spend the most time creating it. I know from experience in my classes, workshops, and private coaching, that we spend most of our profile-building time on this part because it's so important. When it's not you writing about you, it's so much easier to help write a profile headline. That is exactly why many people who may even read this book will opt to use my live workshop and one-on-one coaching options. If you don't currently have the resources for my workshops or coaching services, I usually suggest coming up with three or four different headlines and asking some close friends for their opinions. If you're ambitious, get a good book on marketing headlines to gain some insight into how to write a headline in general. And if you're a real go-getter, use that information to create a couple of kick-butt headlines and test them on two different profiles about you. This is called split testing," and it's a good way to narrow down which headline performs the best. I know this sounds like I'm teaching you marketing skills, and guess what? I am. Remember, my background is in business, and I've always said that you should leave your emotions out of the love search process and treat it more like marketing and promoting yourself. Finding your love at last is not too different from effective business marketing in the sense that you have to know your ideal target client, in this case, your ideal life mate; then you need to know how to communicate that you are here for him or her.

Maybe you don't want 2,874 love prospects contacting you, but you do want as many eyeballs looking at your profile as possible in the hopes that you'll snag the right one.

Headshot and picture:

Spend the money to get it done right. This is an investment in your life, and you are worth it! I was fortunate to have professional photo shots already done. You may never have had any headshots taken in your life. Now is the time. Don't

Designing Your Profile

get too caught up with casual snapshots, pictures with pets, pictures with friends (we all know you have friends, so no need to show them off too), or worse, photos with your ex-husband, ex-wife, ex-girlfriend, ex-lover, etc.!

Here is what I recommend you don't post:

- ♥ A picture of yourself from twenty years ago, prom pictures, or any old photo just to be cute.
- ♥ A picture with your pets, kids, nieces, nephews, family, friends, etc. It's supposed to be about you.
- ♥ Risqué shots of certain parts of your body. Remember, this is for the love of your life, not the love for tonight!
- ♥ An avatar of yourself, even if you're into anime, roleplaying, etc.
- ♥ Pictures of you wearing sunglasses, floppy hats, or anything that hides your face.
- ♥ Half a face. I don't get it when I see one eye and maybe a nose and that's it. If it's art that you are creating, print it off and put it on your refrigerator door. Stick to an honest headshot.
- ♥ Frowns, sad faces, or angry faces. First impressions count. And if it's an angry face, it's the last impression.
- ♥ Someone else's picture. He or she will eventually figure out that you are not the one in the photo.
- ♥ No picture at all. Don't worry; if you're not physically attractive or you don't take a good photo, that's okay because you'll attract your love at last regardless. If

you love yourself, it will come through in your photo and the right person will see the real you.

What you do post:

- ❤ The most recent photo of yourself.
- ❤ A photo of professional quality from someone who knows visually how to pull out your best features. No selfies!

A headshot, full or partial body shot, and personality shots are the three types of photos you should focus on. Even if you carry a few extra pounds, that's okay; that is who you currently are. Love your body and the right person will love you. Your full body should be standing and posed. Take multiple types of headshots from front angles and different side angles. Find a photographer who can capture your personality. If you follow someone on Facebook or other social media who has a photo that captures his or her personality, ask the person who took it. I do this with my different speaker friends. They all have decent pictures of themselves, but you can always tell when someone found the right photographer—the person who really captured the essence of who he or she is visually. That's what you want too.

Capture your personality. If you're playful, show playfulness. If you're athletic, take a photo in your tennis, golf, or volleyball outfit. Be careful in this picture; you don't want to be peg-holed as a tennis player, golfer, or volleyball fanatic. Remember, these are activities that you enjoy, but if you remember from Chapter 2: Knowing Yourself, you are more than what you do. You are first your core characteristics.

Color and/or black and white is okay. Sometimes, photos taken in black and white can express more emotion than color photos. If you like black and white, make sure the photo is taken by someone who specializes in black and white stylings.

If your dating profile system allows more photos, just keep repeating those three main shots of head, body, and personality. Once again, that Fourth of July picnic at Uncle Ned's may have been a fun time, but rarely does an iPhone on a stick capture your essence.

Who You Are:

Use your knowledge about yourself to give someone a clear idea of who you are and the values you hold. If there is room on your profile page, include a short story to illustrate those key points. For example, if you believe in the value of all living things, health, and family, you may have a story that sounds like this:

To understand more of who I am, during my off time, I like taking nature hikes in the local hills like I did with my nieces and nephews last spring. Besides enjoying the outdoors and exercise in general, I find that hiking gives me a chance to connect with nature and Mother Earth. In fact, in this one excursion, we even rescued a baby bird who had fallen out of the nest and protected it from predators on the hunt....

You can see how even a few short sentences within a story can tell the reader more about you than a laundry list of your values and beliefs.

Remember, this is a profile that gives the reader/searcher a taste of who you are. Make it accurate enough to show you off and brief enough to make people want more. Most people are going to have a judgment about you from the headline and photo array. They will skim the profile about your personality, and if it's not off-putting, they will go right to the last part of what you want. This is where you separate the love prospects from the pretenders. You don't want to waste your time apologizing to them for not being their type. Just get it over with in this next part.

What You Want:

Eliminate the pretenders in advance with honesty. Remember, it's not a popularity contest about how many people you can attract; it's attracting the right one! When you write about what you want in a person, use the information that you came up with from your Love by Design™ section in Chapter 3. Because you know what is so important to you, you must be discerning in this part of the profile. If you aren't, you'll attract 2,874 potential suitors like I did until I refined this part of my process. Be honest and to the point about what you want. Make sure you include your "musts" in the list; if no smoking is a must,

Designing Your Profile

make sure it's in there. Don't be afraid to tell someone what you want. You are doing yourself and the other person a big service by being brutally honest now. People who haven't read this book find online dating so exhausting and time-consuming because they don't know what they really want and what person is right for them according to their values and beliefs. They try to find their soulmates as if they were shooting arrows at erratically moving targets.

If you want a person over fifty years old, with children over sixteen, who is an entrepreneur, believes in God, and values family, financial freedom, and health, and takes at least two showers a day, then write it down and begin the manifestation process. Don't shortchange yourself. You deserve exactly what you want and need in life.

By the way, the description I just used in this example was posted in my profile back when I found my love at last. In fact, Jim told me he was attracted to me through my profile for my direct and clear communication about what I wanted—a real turn-on for him.

Contact info:

Remember to have your Google phone number set up along with your dating Gmail account that goes with it. You want that barrier of safety between you and the unknown world of online daters.

Last words on online dating and writing a winning profile.

Remember, this is not a popularity contest. This is not social media where the more friends you have, the better. This is about finding your Mr. or Mrs. Right. Be very clear about that objective when you set up this part. It's very easy to get caught up in wanting to be the most popular person to the point where you stop being yourself and start playing to the crowd. Use this amazing Internet tool for its true purpose—to be the most efficient way to connect you to your love at last. Do your homework first! Complete the exercises provided for each chapter or work with me and my team to make sure you are grounded in who you are and who is the right person for you. It's very easy to get overwhelmed by the vast number of interesting people on any of these dating search engines. That's why you will get the most benefit from the work that you've done with me.

Finally, take your time and enjoy the process. If you do your homework with the focus and passion you'd put into planning a fun vacation, it's very possible that you will find your Mr. or Mrs. Right within ninety days. When you complete your winning profile, choose the right dating website that fits your needs and hold on to your hat because you're going to take off fast. During this time, don't plan on taking up a new hobby, starting a new job, or setting new goals for the year. Give yourself the gift of focus and enjoy the process. After all, you are doing what most people only wish they could do—designing your own soulmate, lover, life partner, best friend, and love at last. Enjoy the ride!

Designing Your Profile

For more FREE information, Dating Hints & Tips, Profile Building Templates, Go To:
www.moreloveforyou.com

CHAPTER FIVE
Launching Your Profile

> Choose to surround yourself with positive people & influences.
>
> — Dr. Renée Gordon

- ❤ What dating website is right for me?
- ❤ Should I maximize my efforts and join more than one dating site?
- ❤ Is there a best time of year to post my profile for success?
- ❤ Is there a best time of the week to post my profile?

Swipe for Mr. Right
What dating website is right for me?

Selecting the right dating website is a pivotal decision on your journey to finding your Mr. or Mrs. Right. The choice depends on your specific preferences, intentions, and what you're seeking in a partner. Here are some considerations to help you determine which dating website is right for you:

Mainstream or Niche: Decide whether you prefer a mainstream dating platform or a niche site that caters to specific interests or demographics. Niche sites can be ideal if you have unique preferences or values.

The Grand Daddy of dating websites, with over 39 million users, is Match.com. Even though they are very mainstream, Match Group owns and operates the largest global portfolio of popular online dating services including Tinder, Meetic, OkCupid, Hinge, Plenty of Fish, OurTime and of course, Match.com. In a sense, they are mainstream and niche all in one because they see the practicality of having niche sites within their organization.

Of course, we have traditional niche websites that attract a specific group like JDate, which serves the Jewish community, OurTime, for an older demographic, The League, specific to young professionals, Veggly, the #1 dating site for vegans, Dig, of course for dog owners, Bristle, for people who love beards, Tastebuds, perfect for music lovers, TeamUp Fitness, dating app that focuses on connecting people through fitness, and Wingman, perfect for people who are tired of swiping for themselves and much more.

Relationship Goals: Clarify your relationship goals. Are you looking for a long-term commitment, casual dating, or something in between? Some platforms are tailored for particular relationship types. Elite Singles and Zoosk are examples of dating apps that supply relationships that matter.

Demographics: Consider the age, location, and background of potential matches. Some dating websites have a broad user base, while others cater to specific age groups or regions. JDate is perfect for people who prefer to find, date, and hopefully marry people that practice the Jewish faith and OurTime, which serves mature men and women singles over 50 plus.

Free or Paid: Decide if you're willing to invest in a paid dating site. Paid platforms often provide more features and tend to attract users more committed to finding a partner. If you're looking for your special life mate, invest into your future with a quality paid dating site. Of course, if your budget is important, do what you've got to do.

Safety and Privacy: Research the safety measures and privacy features of the platform. Ensure your personal information is secure and there are options to report or block users if necessary.

User Experience: Test the usability of the site or app. A user-friendly interface can make the dating experience more enjoyable.

Success Stories: Look for reviews and success stories from people who've found love on the platform. Positive experiences from others can be a good sign. In the same light, when someone tells you about their success story from dating online, always ask which dating app they used and ask them why they liked it. It may be right for you.

Trial Period: Many dating sites offer free trials. Take advantage of these to see if the platform aligns with your preferences before committing. You learn so much more when you check it out first before you invest.

Compatibility Algorithms: Some sites use compatibility algorithms to match you with potential partners based on shared interests and values. I have heard of couples who met on eharmony and were successful in finding love. Don't fall into the trap that someone else is doing all the leg work for you and you don't need to do anything. I would double down by using their compatibility algorithms and prepare as we are doing now.

Ultimately, the right dating website for you will align with your unique desires and relationship goals. By carefully considering these factors, you can make an informed choice that increases your chances of finding the perfect match.

Remember, finding love can be a journey, and the right dating platform can be a valuable tool to use along the way.

Should I maximize my efforts and join more than one dating site?

The question of whether to join more than one dating site is a common dilemma for those navigating the world of online dating. The answer is yes and no. While there's no one-size-fits-all answer, there are several factors to consider when deciding whether to maximize your efforts by joining multiple platforms.

Joining multiple dating sites can expand your pool of potential matches. Different platforms attract various user demographics and preferences, giving you a broader range of options. I have some clients who care about finding someone in their faith, like Christian Mingle but also like the variety of a large, broad range like Match.com. You can still stay focused on your potential suitor as being Christian. One site gives you a different perspective than the others, thus giving you more variety.

Consider the specific features and focus of each dating site. Some are geared towards casual dating, while others emphasize long-term relationships. By joining platforms that align with your relationship goals, you can tailor your efforts to what you're seeking.

While more options can be advantageous, it's essential to manage your time and energy effectively. Juggling multiple platforms can become overwhelming, making it challenging to maintain meaningful connections.

Sometimes, quality outweighs quantity. Focusing your efforts on a single dating site and dedicating time to creating a compelling profile as we are doing here, engaging in conversations, and getting to know potential matches can yield better results than spreading yourself too thin.

Regularly assess the results of your dating efforts. If you find that one platform is consistently more successful in meeting your goals, it might be more effective to concentrate your efforts there.

The decision to join more than one dating site depends on your personal preferences and how well you can manage your time and energy. It's essential to strike a balance between diversifying your options and focusing your efforts on quality connections. Ultimately, the key is to choose a dating strategy that aligns with your goals and enables you to enjoy the journey of finding love.

Is there a best time of year to post my profile for success?

Timing can play a subtle role in the success of your dating profile, but it's important not to overemphasize it. There isn't a universally best time of year to post your dating profile, as dating trends can vary based on location, age, and the specific dating platform you're using.

Launching Your Profile

The time leading up to the holiday seasons ignites a sense of urgency for people to have their Plus 1 in place before family gatherings and work holiday parties. In contrast, once the holiday season is in full gear right after Thanksgiving Day, leave it alone and wait for the next big push. People are too busy by then with family and social functions to check their dating accounts.

Also note, many a client has told me stories leading up to a few weeks till Christmas, where they (in their words) were dumped just so their date didn't have to buy them a holiday gift. As awful as it sounds, they may have done you a great favor long-term by telling you all you need to know about them.

The period right after New Year's is often associated with a surge in online dating activity. Many individuals make resolutions to find love, so early January can be a good time to post your profile. This is also the time that people begin to set up their Valentines date in advance because they made a promise from the year before that they will never be alone on Valentines Day ever again.

February is a month when people are particularly focused on relationships. Posting your profile a few weeks before Valentine's Day can increase your visibility. But as I mentioned above, beginning in January will get you more variety and you and your date won't feel as much pressure to do the normal Valentines Day stuff if you just met. Who wants to buy a seasonally overpriced bouquet of roses for someone that you just met? Don't wait too close to Valentine's Day to find a date. By then, you could have a date but no where to go because they are sold out for the holiday.

The warmer months tend to be more active for outdoor social activities, which can translate to increased online dating. People are more likely to seek connections during these seasons.

The key to a successful dating profile is not the timing but the effort you put into crafting an authentic, engaging, and attractive profile. Consistency in your online interactions and patience are equally vital. Remember that love can be found at any time of the year, so focus on creating a profile that truly represents you and your relationship goals. I always tell my clients that when it happens, it happens, as long as you stay focused and clear about who you are and who you'd like to attract most.

Is there a best time of the week to post my profile?

My engineer types love asking me this question. Here is what I came up with for them. While there's no universal best time of the week to post your dating profile, some strategic considerations can help increase your visibility and potential for success in the world of online dating.

Many dating platforms see increased activity on weekdays, especially Tuesday and Wednesday evenings. People often have more time to browse and interact after work. However, weekends can also be fruitful, as individuals might be more relaxed and open to exploring potential matches.

Mondays can be a busy and stressful time for many people as they start their work week. It might not be the ideal day to make a first impression with your dating profile.

Evening hours, from 7 pm to 10 pm, are generally considered prime time for online dating. This is when people tend to unwind and dedicate time to their personal lives.

Beyond the specific time of the week, consistency in your online presence matters. Regularly checking and updating your profile and engaging with potential matches can improve your chances of success. Remember, this is a commitment to yourself to find your Mr. or Mrs. Right. Stay consistent and make it fun!

If you're in a different time zone from most of your potential matches, it's essential to adapt your posting schedule to align with their online activity times. When I first began my search for Mr. Right, I was open to meeting someone from anywhere in the United States and beyond. It was much more difficult to do this before Zoom became popular. By the way, I had suitors who flew in to meet me for dinner from their home in New York. It's possible to find your love anywhere you choose. Luckily, my love was in California, a one-hour flight or five hours car ride away, much more convenient than flying to and from New York.

Launching Your Profile

The quality of your profile, your interactions, and your genuine connection with potential matches remain more crucial than the timing of your profile posting. Experiment with different days and hours to find what works best for you, but always remember that authenticity and engagement are the keys to online dating success and finding your Mr. Right.

Top 21 Dating Websites

In this report, I've included the most popular dating websites as well as those more specific to culture, age, and religious beliefs. The larger and more popular websites like Match.com include these same cultural, age, and religious belief specifics as well, but if, for instance, your belief is very strong in one religion, culture, or age preference, the specific, overall smaller website may suit you better. For instance, many of my love clients who are Jewish have found much success on JDate.com, even though they were on Match.com as well. You can do the same and join one large site like Match.com and one smaller, more specific dating site if you find one that applies to you.

One word of caution to the person new to dating online: Join only one online dating site at a time. When you're a new member, you will be overwhelmed with requests to meet at the beginning because in the words of another client of mine, "You are fresh meat!" I suggest sticking to one site at first to prevent feeling overwhelmed and having the joy sucked out of your search efforts because the process begins to feel like work.

BlackPeopleMeet.com: The name says it all. This website is devoted to serving black singles. Although it has a smaller user base than other sites like Match.com and eharmony.com, BlackPeopleMeet.com is a growing site exclusively for black and interracial dating.

BuddhistConnect.com: The largest Buddhist website for dating, social networking, and business networking.

BuddhistDatingService.com: "Find Nirvana with someone special" is this site's marketing phrase. Once again, if being with an individual whose belief systems follow Buddhism is important to you, then this may be the right site.

BuddhistPassions.com: Largest free dating and social networking site for Buddhist singles.

Chemistry.com: This is a website devoted to LGBT (Lesbian, Gay, Bisexual, and Transgender) singles to help them find their love at last. This site does most of the work for you through strong personality matching results. Members are limited in their ability to search independently through profiles, so if you like to do the looking yourself, this may not be the site for you. But the site is focused on helping members find long-term love relationships.

ChristianMingle.com: It's obvious from its name that this is a great site for Christian singles looking for other Christian singles. It's user friendly with many interactive features like prayer requests, Bible study, and daily Bible verses. With a growing network of users and over 1 million members currently using the site every month, it is an obvious choice for Christian singles looking for a match.

Dating.com: Innovative communications tools with enhanced security and privacy and of course, personalized match recommendations.

eharmony.com: This site's claim to fame is its scientific approach based on an intensive personality questionnaire for finding love. It also has a focus on Christian singles. It claims that ninety couples a day get married as a result of meeting here.

GreenSingles.com: Yes, it's a place where ecologically minded singles can find like-minded, available, eco-conscious singles. This site is perfect for the person whose values and beliefs are highly driven by making the Earth a better, environmentally healthier place.

JDate.com: This is the number one site for people of Jewish faith to meet other singles of Jewish faith. If finding a person of Jewish faith is one of your most important values, you'll have an easier time here finding someone available to you because of its wide selection.

JustSeniorSingles.com: This free dating site is devoted to fifty-plus mature singles. It also simplifies the online dating process to make it user-friendly, especially for some technology-challenged seniors.

LDSSingles.com: This website is specific to Mormon or Church of Latter-Day Saints (LDS) singles.

Match.com: This was the site I used to find my love at last. It has been around the longest and is still the most popular of all the dating sites serving over 39 million people.

MeninLove.com: This is a local website for gay men to find casual meetups or for dating or finding the loves of their lives.

OKCupid.com: This free site connects LGBT singles for casual meetups or long-term love. As with any free site, you run the risk of meeting people who are less than committed in the search for happily ever after.

OurTime.com: Another popular fifty-plus website for mature singles. It also simplifies the online dating process to make it easy for some technology-challenged individuals.

PlentyofFish.com: POF (as it's referred to by enthusiasts) is one of the largest free websites devoted to finding the love of your life. Once again, this is a simple to operate website that has a phone-friendly app to appeal to our increasing appetite for anything mobile.

SilverSingles.com: Another excellent dating site for men and women over 50+

SingleParentMeet.com: The name says it all—it's a place that focuses on singles with kids, and as the statistics show, that is a growing segment of the dating world. It takes one possible negative disclosure out of the looking process by addressing it upfront. My husband Jim shared with me that in his dating experience in the Silicon Valley area of California, disclosing that you have children was a huge issue for some singles. I can see the value of the approach this website takes. The only thing to address is the question of how many kids you have and how old they are.

Veggly.com: The number one dating app designed for vegans and vegetarians to connect with like-minded individuals who share the same values and lifestyle choices.

Zoosk.com: This is the dating site for the new age of dating, syncing seamlessly with social media and mobile devices. Its claim to fame is its unique behavioral matchmaking capability that improves as you use its website, the theory being that the more you use it, the more likely you'll be to find exactly what you're looking for in a match.

Launching Your Profile

*For more FREE information, Dating Hints & Tips,
Profile Building Templates, Go To:
<u>www.moreloveforyou.com</u>*

CHAPTER SIX
Following Up

"Our greatest weakness lies in giving up.
The most certain way to succeed is
always to try just one more time."

— Thomas A. Edison

- ❤ How do I stay sane during the online search process?
- ❤ How soon should we meet in person?
- ❤ Once there is interest on both sides, what do I do next?
- ❤ How do I incorporate my need to know their values without it sounding like a sales script?

- ❤ Give me an example of how I can incorporate my value and characteristic needs within a question?
- ❤ I get overwhelmed when I'm in the dating process, especially the online dating process. So many people that I'm afraid that I'll miss the right one during the hectic process. How do I avoid that?

How do I stay sane during the online search process?

Yes, it can be overwhelming at the beginning. Any new process seems unmanageable at the onset. I suggest that you don't include launching other goals at the same time you publish your profile or you'll be too overwhelmed and set yourself up for a stressful commencement.

Navigating the online dating process can be exciting, but it can also be a rollercoaster of emotions. Stay sane and maintain your mental and emotional well-being during your love search journey.

Be realistic about what you're seeking and what online dating can offer. Not every connection will lead to love, and that's perfectly normal. Understand that rejection is part of the process. In fact, I share with my clients that rejection is the natural way to eliminate non-matches from the get-go. Remember, you are looking for that one special person and understand that this is not a popularity contest. As I mentioned previously in this book, I was not fortunate at the beginning of my love search journey and I had thousands of interested parties wanting my attention all at once. I quickly refined my process to pre-eliminate gentlemen by becoming more specific to my needs from Mr. Right. I wish I had done that sooner. It would have saved me much time.

While it's essential to be active on dating platforms, don't let it consume your life. Set boundaries for your screen time to prevent burnout and maintain a healthy balance with your offline activities. I usually suggest creating a healthy habit of 20 minutes per day then shutting it down. This allows you to keep up with new people tapping my shoulder and gives me 10 minutes to check out new possibilities. This balanced approach allows you to take care of your physical and emotional well-being. Engage in activities you enjoy, exercise, meditate, and seek support from friends and family.

Be cautious when sharing personal information, and always meet new acquaintances in public places. Trust your instincts and report any suspicious behavior on the platform. Make sure that you create a new free email account specific to your love search efforts like a gmail account. Your gmail account includes an attached phone number for further security. I'm not suggesting that you become paranoid but do yourself a favor and be extra vigilant out there.

Finding the right match can take time, so be patient. Avoid rushing into relationships out of frustration or loneliness.

I suggest that you meditate for at least every minute that you spend online checking your dating site. When you meditate, focus on the person that you described in your manifestation decree. It will both calm you down and prevent frustration as well as activate your Reticular Activation System.

Be authentic and true to yourself in your profile and interactions. Authenticity attracts genuine connections and helps you filter out incompatible matches. If you're not operating in the present and feel that you're missing out, you may want to push yourself onto someone. If doing that doesn't make you feel good, imagine how it makes the other person feel. Expect ups and downs. Rejection or disappointing interactions are part of dating, and developing resilience is key to staying sane.

If you feel overwhelmed or fatigued, it's okay to take breaks from online dating. Recharge and return with a fresh perspective. Share your experiences and feelings with friends, family, or a therapist. Talking to others can provide valuable insights and emotional support. Above all, have fun during the process.

Finally, use each interaction as a learning opportunity. Reflect on what you've discovered about yourself and your preferences along the way. When you don't expect anything, you become more present, and you present yourself in a much more authentic and relaxed way.

Staying sane means maintaining a sense of balance, resilience, and self-care. By managing expectations, practicing patience, and seeking support when needed, you can navigate the online search process with your well-being intact and increase your chances of finding the right match for you.

How soon should we meet in person?

Ah, the "let's jump in with both feet" approach. Two words, Be Cool. Dating is all part of the process of attracting your own Mr. or Mrs. Right. I like to describe it as letting everything unfold the way it should happen. Nothing forced ever works out. So Be Cool and let them come to you.

I often equate dating to fishing (why not, everyone uses the term, "There are more fish in the sea." when consoling someone who lost a good possible date). If you are fishing, usually you put some yummy bait onto the fishing line. This is your headshot and profile. Then you drop the line into the water and let it become known to all the other fish. That's being patient. Then you tug on the line a bit to tease the fish, but not too much, just enough to make it interesting. This is being cool and not overreacting or over expecting something to happen. You usually get your fish on the line when you are not thinking about it. You just let the line do its thing and your manifestation process will lead the right fish to you when you least suspect it.

In the next chapter, we outline your process, step by step. No guesswork involved.

Once there is interest on both sides, what do I do next?

Talk to them. I know, scary huh. But that's what you do. After the flirtatious first contact method, which for most dating apps is a text of some kind, suggest a quick phone call to hear a voice on the other end. But before we continue the step-by-step, I want to introduce you to this new method.

The Stop Light Method:

At every step along this process, you ask yourself is this person worth going on to the next step (green light) or take a day or two to think about it (yellow light) or they just don't match my manifestation letter (red light). To reiterate, red light means stop, yellow light, slow down and evaluate, or green light, it's safe to go now. If the profile that you read seems like a green light, here is the next process:

- ❤ Arrange a short call, 20 minutes - what light, green, yellow, or red?
- ❤ Arrange a longer call, up to an hour - where are we now?
- ❤ If it's a yellow light, arrange another call.

How the "Traffic Light Process" works:

At the end of each action, if you immediately feel good about the call or meeting, then schedule the next action. If you feel any apprehension, it means your inner voice is warning you to be cautious. Repeat the same call or meeting until you are ready to proceed with more information or learn something that causes you to stop and end the progress.

Here is a chart if you are in an ideal place that shows green all the way.

Steps to Finding Your Soulmate:

Next Action	Green	Yellow	Red
Arrange a short phone call, no more than 20 minutes			
Arrange a longer phone call, up to 60 minutes			
Arrange a Zoom or Team video call and schedule 20 minutes			
Arrange a second Zoom or Team video call and schedule 40 minutes			
Meet for coffee or juice in person, schedule short 30-40 minutes			
Meet again for coffee or juice in person, longer 50-60 minutes			
Meet for lunch for a first time			
Meet for lunch or brunch for a second meal			
Meet for dinner (repeat dinner/lunch at least five times before committing to meeting his family or going away for a weekend) remember, if it's right, it's right. He or she won't go away because you are not intimate yet. Be Cool			

My Favorite Dating Tool!

Yes, my favorite dating tool is (drum roll please) Zoom! I wish my husband and I had that tool. It would have reduced the confusion and anxiety for our first in person date by a long shot. Remember in my story of meeting my Mr. Right (yes that's my husband Jim), our wires got crossed and I never went to his website to learn more about him including what he looked like. It wasn't until eight weeks after our first phone call that he confirmed what I looked like and the first time, including photos, that I learned what he looked like. I never doubted my intuition that he was the right one. It did make me a bit nervous not knowing when driving to our first face-to-face date.

After the pandemic in 2020, we all know how to use Zoom and the app is free on your computer, tablet, or phone. A variety of virtual meeting products have tried to fill the need, including Microsoft Teams, Skype, Webex, Google Meet and GoToMeeting, but Zoom has been one of the major players with a dominant market share which means that most people know how to use it. The free version does limit you to at most 40 minutes per meeting but there is a trick to continue staying on the meeting over 40 minutes which I will not share with you today because it's not relevant for our uses today.

So why is Zoom such a great dating tool?

Most people feel that they need to rush to see what the other person really looks like, right? We all know that photos can be brushed up a bit and what self-respecting gal doesn't want to always look her best anyway. So here is the skinny on why Zoom is such a great dating tool. It protects you from yourself. Yes, I said it. It protects you from jumping in with two feet and wasting time and money going on a date that is uncomfortable at best.

Remember the fishing story? Be patient. This process allows you to cover more ground by talking to more people and not wasting your time meeting for coffee. After all, how much coffee can one person drink anyway?

I digress. Use the Stop Light method to ask a few select questions that we'll go over later in this book. The first phone call confirms that they are intelligent enough to pick up a phone and mumble a few words. The second phone call is longer and provides you with the ability to ask your Key Probing Questions (more on that later in this book, I promise). If they still pass the muster from your key probing questions, then they get a Green light and move on to a short Zoom meeting.

Zoom meeting #1: This is where you are polite and let them ask a few questions. Remember, they may have read my book too and need to ask their probing questions. But while they are talking, look at their background. Hopefully they don't have that nasty blurred background. But look at what is behind them. If it's a bookshelf, what kind of books they read. Also, while you are on Zoom, snag a screenshot of this person. It may come in handy when you're trying to remember who you talked to this week. Trust me, it can get confusing if you don't do these tricks to remember who's who in the zoo!

When you are on your first Zoom meeting, look at how they are dressed and whether their fingernails are clean and clipped. These are good indicators of their general hygiene. If you can tell things look good, end your meeting at 20 minutes. Tease the person by giving them just enough of you. If you schedule another Zoom, make this for the full time of 40 minutes. Once again, stick to the plan. Even if you have a paid business account that can go 30 hours straight on Zoom, don't tell them that. Stick to a maximum of 40 minutes.

By the way, all during this time, we may be communicating between meetings with texting but only to confirm times and links to where you'll be next. Let them know up front that you'll be using texting just for scheduling and not conversation. You see, a conversation is really two ways. Texting truly is only a one-way conversation.

If you are at an impasse and you're not sure whether to meet in person or not, schedule another Zoom meeting for 40 minutes maximum. If they agree, they are interested. You see how this works. You control your time and money by not going out all day meeting people at your local coffee shop. If there is anything that we learned from the pandemic it's that we can do quite a bit from our desk and computer.

The time has come. The lights are all green for go. It's now time to meet for coffee or juice. Yes, once again, limit your first meeting to 20-30 minutes. You can even have a friend call you at the beginning of your meeting in case they are nasty and not representative of how they showed themselves on camera. If you need an excuse to go, take the call and politely leave. If you are a Green light, it's a go and just reply with a text saying that you'll call later. Make sure that your Key Probing Questions are still weaved into your conversations and now that you've met them in person, check out those fingernails to see how well they are groomed.

If it's still a Green go, keep going down the list. Don't be tempted to rush the process. Everyone has paid the price. I'm trying to save you time and money by not going on dates that should have never been. But more important, once you find those red flags, it's easier to hang up or click off a Zoom than leave a restaurant or even their house!

After you've gone to a few dinners as a couple, you can start meeting friends and even family. By this time, you're becoming comfortable with each other. Now you haven't been intimate, have you? As much as you'd like, remember, this is not dating to find a conquest. This is about you being ready to find or attract that special person that you want to spend the rest of your life with together. Be Cool! You'll get intimate soon enough.

The 3-Month Rule:

If you've made it past three months as an exclusive couple, congratulations! This is the first major milestone in your relationship with this person! Now, if you haven't put your dating account on pause, what are you waiting for? Get yourself off the dating site before your new sweetheart's brother or sister finds them still online seemingly looking. Not a good look for you. So put it on pause now!

Within a three-month period, most couples have behaved, meaning, nothing too sensational has happened yet. Now life starts happening. Birthdays, weddings, deaths, even marriages. After three months, your guard goes down and you begin to act like who you really are without the masks. Now the relationship has begun. Now you're getting a sense of who this person you've been with is now acting like who they've been underneath all the niceties. When you've gone through Christmas or a high holiday unscathed, you have a chance. Go Green!

> ***How do I incorporate my need to know their values without it sounding like a sales script?***

A good sales script doesn't sound like a sales script, just like when an accomplished actor reads their script, it sounds like a real person talking. This is how it's done.

Swipe for Mr. Right

Remember Chapter 2? This is where you began to get to know yourself on the inside. Maybe you already knew yourself. Let's say you got reintroduced to what is most important in your life. Then in Chapter 3, we began our Manifestation Decree by designing our Mr. Right. I'll use myself as the example to best explain your sales script to sorting your Mr. Right from the rest of pack.

God is my top value. That means that when I was looking for my Mr. Right years ago (over 23 years to be exact), I knew I needed to be with someone to recognized that God the True Source was present in our daily lives. I could come out and be very direct, but I wanted our first evaluation meetings to be conversational and educational.

Remember, with Jim, I didn't have the opportunity to see what he looked like. He wasn't on the dating website that I was on. During our first contact by phone, I miswrote the URL of his website that he said would tell me all about him, his work, his passions, his history, and his physical appearance. That didn't happen and our conversations were so rich that I forgot to ask him to spell out his URL again for me. During one of our first conversations, I asked him, "What are you doing this Sunday?" He responded that after doing some chores, he had plans to take his son out to shoot hoops followed by a bowl of Vietnamese noodles. I followed up with, "Don't you go to church on Sundays?" Now I wasn't interested if he went to church or not, I just wanted to see if he believed in a higher power.

Jim responded, "No, not this Sunday. Occasionally I'll try out a non-denominational church with a friend or when my parents visit, we'll go to a Catholic Church nearby. I hope it's not a problem that I'm not a church goer. I consider myself more spiritual, meaning I believe in a higher power in God, and I am definitely on a spiritual path. I pray and meditate daily and know that God is there to guide me within my life. How about you, do you go to church?

Without being cold and analytical, I was able to learn more about Jim from that one question instead of asking him, "God, thumbs up or thumbs down?" We had a conversation that was guided by these value probing questions.

This is one of core examples to show you how to get to know more about your date when having a conversation with them. It's okay to pepper in some hobby, interest, and sport questions because that is relevant to who your potential love interest is all about. From asking him if he believes in God, I also found out that he is a family man and that his son is very important to him. Family is my second most important value so that was another thumbs up for Jim. Then he mentioned that he was going to play basketball with his son. That told me that he wasn't a couch potato playing video games and letting his body go to waste. He is an athlete with an athlete mindset, which I like. It's not on my top five list of values, but I still like it. Then he told me that he was going to enjoy a bowl of Vietnamese noodles with his son which told me that he was adventurous with food (boy is he, as I found out later) which is for me part of my value of family that includes doing family type things like cooking and/or eating together. From one thought out question, I learned plenty. Definitely a Green light go! In fact, it's been a Green light go for the past 23 years together.

So go back to your list of your top values. Take one value at a time and make a question out of it like I did. Make it a type of question that would fit within a typical first, second and third date. Why is this important to do at the onset? What do you think? Exactly, you don't want to waste your time and his or her time either. You're doing you and him (or her) both a favor by outlining five to seven key probing questions and working them into your conversation. Typically, most dates are purely social and flirtatious. Save that until you find out if they qualify to be a possible right match for you. Use your first phone and Zoom dates to see if they are green-lighted to eventually meet in person. We all get dazzled with meeting new potential lovers. We get all flustered and let our hormones get the better of us. The Red Light process will help you stay focused at the task at hand instead of doing what most of us have done in the past, which is to…

Look at his or her photo, think they are cute or hot. Connect, make a coffee date and feel the chemistry. Then immediately go to lunch, then dinner then well you know, nature takes over. Then he or she stops calling you and you do it all over again unless they are really good in bed, and you have just developed your new hobby until something happens that brings you down to earth. Is this what you want? Of course not. This is why you're reading this book, because you want to have a life and a relationship with what you have considered your Mr. or Mrs. Right!

How you can create your own Key Probing Questions:

Your Top Value (example) _____God_____

Matching Key Probing Question:

<u>What are you planning to do this Sunday?</u>

Now use your core values instead of using mine to form your questions. Go for it. Don't worry about doing it wrong. The fact is that this direction is leading your questions, you'll do just fine. So go do that now!

Your Top Value _____

Matching Key Probing Question: _____
_____
_____

Your Top Value _____

Matching Key Probing Question: _____
_____
_____

Swipe for Mr. Right

Your Top Value _____

Matching Key Probing Question: _____
_____
_____

Your Top Value _____

Matching Key Probing Question: _____
_____
_____

Your Top Value _____

Matching Key Probing Question: _____
_____
_____

I get overwhelmed when I'm in the dating process, especially the online dating process. There are so many people that I'm afraid that I'll miss the right one during this hectic process. How do I avoid that?

Breathe and take it one person at a time. No rush. The perfect person will show up when you are ready. What's great about this dating process is that it's really an evaluation process. Most dating, without a plan, will carry on and on and you'll rely on those things that you relied on in the past that always attracted Mr. Wrong again and again. No more!

Following Up

One thing we talk about that is important to share with you right now is to understand what we call being in the flow. The flow is a state that transports you from one step of the process to the next in a seamless fashion. To get you into this place you need to focus on writing and reading your Manifestation Letter or Manifestation Decree at least every day. Read it like you've already connected with your Mr. Right. You got it, I'm asking you to imagine that it's a year or two in the future and you're looking back at your relationship with your Mr. Right. Now you're describing him/her like you've already met him or her. I know, you might think I'm crazy, but this works.

The first thing it accomplishes is that you are telling your brain that you have already found your Mr. Right. That immediately removes any fears or anxieties towards the dating process. It also eliminates your overwhelm because, once again, you've already found your Mr. Right so everything now is cool. Aaah.

Wait, are you becoming a buzz kill and the logical part of your thinking is alerting you that this is all a ruse? You haven't found your Mr. Right and life is caving in on itself. You'll be alone forever and the only companions that you'll ever have are rescued cats.

Stop it!

Really, what story do you choose to be part of? The story that tells you that you've already found your Mr. Right or the one where you're taking care of stray cats for the rest of your life?

Of course, you want the first story. The one where all your dreams come true. Let your mind do all the heavy lifting. All you do is relax and be in the flow of your life.

Let me share with you my Manifestation Decree so you understand what I mean:

I value God, Family, Love, Security and Freedom. I am so excited to have found my Mr. Right. He is all that he could be for me. I look back to when we first met, and it was magical. It was so wonderful to learn so much about him without even knowing what he looked like, what car he drove or for even a long time, what he did for a living. I felt his heart and that is all I really needed to know.

This past year has be the best year of my life. I finally know what it feels like to be free and committed to my best friend. I love being with him and he with me. We are like two kids on a never-ending adventure that opens new and exciting opportunities along the way. I feel like I found my place in life and all the knowledge, experience and goals brought me to him.

We have traveled both for work and for pleasure, but to be truthful, it's all been pleasurable. My baby Bianca puppy looks to him like no other person she has looked at before. She feels safe and secure with a man that I feel the same about. Our lives had quickly merged and we're already talking about marriage. After all, that is the next logical step for two people who have finally found out what committed love truly can be. We take time daily to meditate and pray. We take care of our bodies by going to the gym, going on walks, and playing sports. He is an entrepreneur like my Dad and it gives me joy to contribute my own business sense and wisdom to him to give him a different perspective advantage. Finally, I don't have to apologize about my desire for personal development because he loves to grow his life as much as I do.

Holidays have become more special because I share them with my family and his. We have already experienced Christmas and New Years together and they were both magical. I feel like a kid again and love holding hands as we walk our life together. Thank you, God for blessing us both be bringing us together. I promise that I'll be grateful every day that we are together.

Now take out your notebook or journal and write your own Manifestation Decree as if it has already happened.

By the way, this is what I wrote before I met my husband Jim many years ago. I called this letter my letter to God. This was a shortened version of it after I had written my original letter that was 57 pages long. Write like it's already happened and read it at least once a day.

Tell your unconscious self that everything is wonderful with my Mr. Right in my life. You see, your mind doesn't know if this story is going to happen or that it has already happened. Who cares if that in reality it hasn't really happened. It puts you in a more empowered state and it engages your Reticular Activation System (RAS) and builds up your attraction vibrations and frequencies to bring to you, your Mr. Right!

For more FREE information, Dating Hints & Tips, Profile Building Templates, Go To:
www.moreloveforyou.com

Following Up

CHAPTER SEVEN
Closing the Deal

> Listen more than you talk. Nobody learned anything by hearing themselves speak.
>
> — Richard Branson

- ❤ How will I know that I've found the right one for me?
- ❤ When do I sleep with this person?
- ❤ When do I meet his family and friends?
- ❤ If he proposes to me, how do I know it's right. Is there a standard time frame to say "Yes"?

❤ Is it a good idea for us to live together once we get engaged?

Congratulations! If you've made it this far and you've followed the process. I'm guessing that you have or you're very close to finding your own Mr. or Mrs. Right and you are beside yourself with joy.

How will I know that I've found the right one for me?

Recognizing that you've found the right one for you in the realm of relationships is a deeply personal and often intuitive experience. While there's no universal checklist, some signs can indicate that you've discovered a meaningful connection. Compatibility comes when you share some core values, life goals, and have mutual respect for each other's beliefs. Your compatibility extends beyond shared interests to align with fundamental principles.

Emotional connection happens when you feel a strong emotional bond, a sense of comfort, and a deep understanding with this person. Your conversations are meaningful, and you can be your authentic self.

Dolores and Joe, my mother and father-in-law, had that deep emotional connection even when during the last few years of their lives together, they no longer lived in the same apartment at their luxury elderly care facility. My mother-in-law's dementia progressed to where they needed to protect her from possibly leaving the facility unsupervised, so she was put into memory care, which was a separate building near my father-in-law's apartment. Even though they spent their last 18 months separate from each other, except when Joe would visit Dolores, they could feel each other and not feel apart during that time.

Effective communication means that you and your partner communicate openly and honestly. You feel heard and valued. Conflicts are resolved through healthy dialogue and compromise. As I frequently say, women need love and men need respect. Honoring each other's perspective and point of view becomes a cornerstone to your long-lasting relationship.

Growth in your relationship encourages both personal and mutual growth. You support each other's aspirations and challenges, fostering self-improvement. Many times, we stop what we are doing to support the other.

This book would not make it to you without the help of my husband Jim, who is an expert in both project management and book publishing. We are each other's biggest fans, and that support is extremely important to your relationship. Unconditional support means the right one for you is your biggest cheerleader. They stand by you through thick and thin, providing unwavering support and encouragement.

The shared warmth of being together brings joy and happiness. You share laughter, experiences, and create positive memories. In fact, I've noticed how we attract other couples just like us. You too will experience that the more you be your happy, joyful self. You will attract couple friends just like you. One of my visions is for a world free of divorce and broken marriages. All change begins with me. The more that we attract more couples like us, the more that energy affects and inspires more to be happy and joyful.

Trust and respect are the foundation of your relationship. You are with the right one when you feel safe and secure with that person, and your boundaries are honored. You are not two halves that now make a whole. Rather you are two that generate more together like the equation of $1 + 1 = 3+$!

Both of you envision a future together, and your long-term goals align seamlessly. It may not be exact, but when you get excited about the other person's future vision, you know it was just a matter of time before you would have discovered the vision for yourself.

You achieve consistency in that the right one's actions match their words. Their love is consistent, not based on fluctuating moods or circumstances. I saw that with my business coach and mentor Eric Lofholm. We jokingly refer to him as "Steady Eddy" or I should say, "Steady Eric", no rhyme, but you get what we are saying. Eric was consistent before he met his Queen Heather (yes, his words) and he is consistent after they finally met and got married. Eric is man of his word and that means so much in building respect and love within a couple. You already have that or you're reaching towards that level of consistency. Hang on to this person tight.

Gut feeling completes the package that yells at you that it's right. Sometimes, it's that simple. You have an inner knowing that this person is the one you want to spend your life with.

Edward was a mess when he was recovering from his divorce. With my help he began to accept happiness into his life. He came to me one day to tell me that he thinks he has found the one. And as much as I tried to convince him that he couldn't be ready yet, he kept telling me I was wrong. All he kept saying was that his gut kept telling him that she is the one and that it didn't make sense, but emotionally he felt it. He asked her Dad for her hand in marriage, got married and soon after they had a daughter they named after me, Renée. This has been over nine years ago and they are happier than they could ever be. Your intuition knows. Follow your gut every time.

Ultimately, discovering the right one for you is a journey of self-awareness and relationship growth. It's about finding a partner who complements and enhances your life, creating a deep and lasting connection filled with love, trust, and shared dreams. Trust your instincts, nurture your relationship, and know that the right one will bring out the best in you, just as you do in them.

How soon do I sleep with this person?

Deciding when to become intimate with someone is a highly personal choice, and there is no one-size-fits-all answer. Much like the question, how do you know it's the one? You just know.

The timing of physical intimacy in a relationship should align with your comfort, consent, and the mutual readiness of both partners. I believe that if you base your decision from love, not just lust or it's not based on your ego (it's been a blank, blank long time).

Communicate with each other first. I know, it doesn't work like this in movies. But hey, nothing works like it does in the movies. That's why it's called entertainment. Open and honest communication is key. Discuss your feelings and boundaries with your partner. Make sure you both have a clear understanding of each other's expectations. Within my couple love coaching program, we talk about our 5-Day Foreplay™ Plan that encourages anticipation foreplay to build up the actual sexual event. We're not going to talk about that today, but it is a love tactic that has been very popular with both sexes. Women love it because it's a process that takes into consideration a woman's need to prepare both the physical act of love making and the emotional. Guys like it because guys like anything that has to do with sex. Sorry guys, you know it's true.

Closing the Deal

Forming an emotional connection. Many people prefer to wait until they've established a strong emotional connection with their partner. Feeling safe, loved, and understood can enhance the experience. Feeling safe is the precursor to trust and that is essential in choosing to make love the first time. Both partners should enthusiastically agree to any physical activity. Consent is a continuous process, meaning it can be withdrawn at any time. Which brings us full circle. Emotional connection creates safety, which builds trust, that leads to consent which continues in a loving circle.

Personal values must be reconsidered by both parties. Consider your own values and beliefs regarding physical intimacy. What feels right for you may not align with societal norms, and that's perfectly okay. You began this journey with your core values and beliefs. It makes sense that you should continue to make your decisions in this way.

John and Rachel began their relationship just the way that I suggested, no in-person date until you've passed the phone calls and Zoom meeting stages. They had no problem with all of that because they were five to six hours away by car. They took advantage of the long-distance relationship to get to know each other very well. When they first met each other, there was a strong appreciation for each other as people first which means they respected each other. The conversation about intimacy came up in normal conversation, which made it open and honest, a good safe beginning. John made it clear that he had strong physical desires with Rachel but honored their relationship too much to push it. John used the term that his intention was to be in the long game and waiting was no problem if it meant that the result was being together forever.

When she stayed over at his house one time, she saw how he had given his bed to Rachel while he prepared sleeping arrangements for himself on a futon in the family room. Not feeling pressured allowed Rachel to feel safe in his home. And as it happened, she invited him to join her in a bath together because she was ready and that made all the difference in the world for the both of them. It wasn't planned to happen this way and it probably came sooner than they planned. That is why it happened, because she was comfortable first.

Remember, there is no right or wrong time to sleep with someone; it's about what feels right for you and your partner. Trust your instincts, prioritize open communication, and focus on mutual consent and comfort. Physical intimacy should enhance your connection, and when the timing is right, it can be a beautiful and meaningful part of your relationship. Trust me when I say that when it's right for the both of you, you're so glad you waited. As the saying goes, it is worth the wait!

Closing the Deal

When do I meet his or her family and friends?

Consider kids, different for young and old. Share your stuff but don't imprint your beliefs onto other people and make them wrong. But do point out your thought process for YOU so they understand that they need to make those same decisions too.

Let me answer this question with a couple of stories:

Jack started dating this attractive mom of three children, two girls and one boy. Their ages ranged between 9 (boy) to 13 and 16 years of age. The mom was pushing her kids into the picture early because she figured that if they didn't like Jack, she didn't want her heart to be broken if they didn't like him later. As much as it seemed logical, it didn't work out. The kids loved Jack. This confirmed her feelings for Jack as well. But the part that she never considered was Jack. He liked her kids but felt too overwhelmed by the instant family. Too much, too soon. She learned a valuable lesson, confirm your love for each other first. Make sure that you're both on the same page before you take a huge step like introducing your kids. Your kids love you unconditionally and if your union formed under common core characteristics first, they will learn to love you as well.

The second story was with Ruby and Juan. They both followed my system by meeting online. Ruby was always concerned that if the right guy came into her life that she didn't want what happened in the past when she left a relationship with a broken heart because she left the kids too. Ruby made peace with herself that the guy that she was seeing wasn't a match for her. But his children were a match. Awkward! Heartache ensued for both Ruby and the two children. To avoid this happening again, she wrote in her profile, "Kids 16 years and older accepted." Juan had one boy 16 1/2 years old. Ruby and Juan have been together for years and their son is on his own but considers them all family.

Bottom line, it's important to take your kids into consideration when you are looking for a new husband or wife. Take into consideration the impact on them first before you begin your search for your Mr. Right. When you do begin the dating process, keep them separate before you introduce them to each other.

With friends, it's a bit easier but still needs consideration too. Friends are happy if you're happy, but make sure you are both sure about each other's emotional wellbeing first. If you are solid emotionally, you'll be okay if one of your respective friends brings up a crazy boy or girl friend from the past. You know they'll do that to you. They can't help but compare the new person in your life to the former, like, "Hey she doesn't seem as crazy as that girl Jill. Remember her. Do ya, do ya?" Yes, it's happened.

Finally, parents. If your parents are still alive and well, there will be a family function that you all will be at together. Wherever you are in your relationship should be what you reveal to your parents. Simple and to the point. If you've made it this far, unless something drastic happens, it's likely that the next big event will be your own wedding. It's important you both have a conversation before you and the family get together, lay it all out so they don't have to wonder and guess what kind of relationship you have with each other. Parents are much more cool than you think they are. Basically, all they care about is that you are happy. If you are happy, tell them and they'll be fine.

If he proposes to me, how do I know it's right. Is there a standard time frame to say "Yes"?

Determining whether a proposal is right and the ideal time to say "Yes" are significant decisions that should be based on your unique circumstances, feelings, and compatibility with your partner.

I know for me, saying yes nine times before meant I had to be extra super certain I was ready to say yes to engagement #10. Fortunately, engagement #10 was with Jim, who is my husband. I may have blown the punchline, but that's okay. He was aware of the nine other engagements that went astray, so he knew what he was getting into. To be totally honest, I told Jim that I was ready on Christmas Day, during our first vacation together on the Big Island of Hawaii. I basically said, "Trade me or play me. What is it?"

This was my response to his card where he wrote the following:

> "Love does not consist in gazing at each other, but in looking outward together in the same direction."
>
> — Antoine de Saint-Exupery

I guess, now that I look back, that was kind of romantic. But remember, I wasn't getting any younger. I didn't want to waste any more of my pretty with someone who wasn't serious. Obviously, he was serious.

Anyway, Jim agreed that we should explore more to make sure that it's right for us for the right reasons. We booked a weekend marriage preparation session. It was run by the Catholic Church at a beautiful mansion in Malibu Beach hills.

Jim kept saying that we weren't quite ready, but soon. He was big saying that we would know the right time when it came. I thought he was stalling but I guess I figured he was worth trusting until we completed this pre-marriage counseling. It didn't happen until we came to the end of the weekend session, when we had to write a letter to our respective sweetheart.

By the way, usually these pre-marriage weekend sessions are only reserved for people who are already engaged. We attended it to prepare for getting engaged. Made sense to us.

Back to the letter. This was my epiphany. I began to write the same stuff that everyone else would write. Then it hit me. The reason why Jim had suggested this whole weekend process finally took hold. He knew me well enough that he knew I would get it even if it took all weekend to finally get to me. I then went back to him to share my love letter to him.

I took his hand with my hand and held my letter in the other hand. I began with a lot of love talk I'm not sharing with you today. But near the end of the letter I confessed, "...and I agree, we are not quite ready for marriage, but we will be very soon." Just then I really understood the poem that Jim gave to me months earlier and realized that he was basically saying to me that we are going to be married no matter what. His plans are now my plans and vice versa. We were now on the same page and not engaged.

Three months later, 9/11 hit when Jim was staying with me at my place. He and I had just completed a training program for one of his corporate clients the day before and we woke to a day that changed our country and how we lived forever. We reacted probably as you did but a couple of weeks later, we were still together. He had his SUV and he had another training to do the next week, so I went with him. We stayed together a total of three weeks straight. The night before I had to get back to my home in Southern California, we talked. We both said simultaneously that it was time to make this relationship permanent and get married.

As sad as it was to experience the tragedy of 9/11, it made us realize one very real thing. We didn't know what life was going to present to us. We could only live in the present and one of the most important questions we had to ask ourselves was, "How do we want to spend our time together?" The answer was, we wanted to spend it together. We were married seven months later and have been together since July 8th, 2000. No more than a few days at a time separated us during all those years. Every time that we celebrate milestones and success or setbacks or deaths, we always look at each in the eye and say, "I'm so glad that we are here to experience this together."

Jim refers to this as the non-engagement wedding just to emphasize that we had to break the pattern and go right from sweethearts to marriage and skip the engagement business since it didn't seem necessary. As you can see, we just knew that this was the right move for both of us. No hesitation. No ego. No other reason except to experience a loving life together and to continue the adventure that we began when we first met.

So here is the good news. The Swipe for Mr. Right process is so real and authentic that when you first meet in person, you are far further along in your relationship than most people who are already engaged. We should know because we spent a whole weekend together at a pre-marriage counseling seminar. Remember how I told you that unknown to the organizers, we were the only couple that was not already engaged? The rest of the couples, and there had to be about 75 total couples, were already engaged. In fact, for some of them, this was the very last step before they tied the knot. You see, in the Catholic Church, you were required to complete this weekend class and you had to pass to get a certificate to present to the priest that was to marry you. We didn't care if we got that little piece of paper. We were there for each other. We cared so much about each other that our love, respect, and care was the only important thing to us.

What was so interesting was that most of the other couples believed that we were one of the counselors running the weekend seminar. They all believed we were some kind of plant within all the other couples. Our take on love, marriage and sharing a life with each other was profoundly more advanced than any couple there. Now I don't say this to brag but to illustrate that the one couple that was not engaged was the one that was perceived as one of the leaders of the whole seminar. It got so humorous that some of the seminar leader couples would refer to us when they were stumped with a relationship question. The teachers. The ones that we were supposed to learn from this weekend.

The point is that we were humble enough and valued greatly the concept of committing our lives to each other that we looked to take a whole weekend to get any idea that would give us an advantage in staying together forever.

If you didn't get this question answered by our love story. Let me summarize:

There is no reason why you need to be together. You are totally whole and have greatness within you. But remember the poem/quote that my husband Jim gave to me that I really understood only after we devoted a weekend to premarital instruction. Let go of your preconceived ideas of love as only the attractive, physical element and gaze towards a life to experience together. When you look at that other person and you say, if I only have one day on this earth, who do I want to spend it with? If your answer is the person that you've been courting these last few months or years, there you go, you've got your answer. Then each day of your life, begin and end the day with gratitude for each other and ask yourself this question each day: "Who would I love to share this next day with completely." You should know the answer by now. Good luck and be comfortable with the fact that the method that helped you find each other is also the one that is going to keep you together.

For more FREE information, Dating Hints & Tips, Profile Building Templates, Go To:
www.moreloveforyou.com

Closing the Deal

CHAPTER EIGHT
The Transition

> The secret of change is to focus all of your energy not of fighting the old, but on building the new.
>
> —Socrates

- ❤ What should I expect life to be like after I'm engaged to be married?
- ❤ How do I transition easily from being single to couples' life?
- ❤ I've focused so much on attracting my Mr. or Mrs. Right that I feel stuck in that mode. How do I change it?

- ❤ Do I help my new significant other to transition too?
- ❤ What should I expect life to be from now on?

What should I expect life to be like after I'm engaged to be married?

Remember, you are both still the same people that you were when you first met. The difference now is that you are transitioning from the ME to the WE and it can be awkward during this period to know how one is to act. So don't act, just BE. Life between engagement and marriage should be just like any day. Change is slow and deliberate, but it's still change.

Because you've found each other through our process that relies heavily on knowing and attracting someone who shares many common core characteristics, you are further along than most people. You see, you've already began building your relationship on a solid foundation. Now you keep doing it. It doesn't have to be all at once, as transformation to a bonafide couple takes time. In fact, true masters will usually say something like this next statement.

"The more I know, the more I realize what I don't know."

Wisdom says that knowing is done over a lifetime. My first bit of advice is not to worry. Make this a lifetime project for two. Show daily improvement and let that success compound over the weeks, months, and years together.

The Transition

There is a story about a breakfast of eggs and bacon and the part that a hen and a pig play in that role. The hen was involved because it supplied the eggs. But the pig was committed. You are no longer involved in a relationship. That term is usually used when you are dating or having regular sex with someone. It is an appropriate word because without commitment, you are just close friends. Once you take that step to saying to your sweetheart that you can't imagine life without them being in it, you are committed.

Conversations about the future will become more prevalent than before you were engaged. You'll have important discussions about your life together, including living arrangements, finances, career goals, and family planning. These conversations are crucial for aligning your expectations and goals. For some people, this can be unnerving. Up to now, your life goals were your own life goals. Now you're with another. For most, nothing may change at all. I know with Jim and I, we began to morph into each other's goals. Now, we share our goals as we go along. You see before, when your goals were your own, people would cheer you on from the outside, but not support them from the inside. When I get approached to do a TV show, one of my many important goals, I know that Jim will be there to support me in any way that I need him to support me. I may not be as automatic at first, but it will be as you share life more.

I also know that wedding planning comes up very quickly. Expect to dive into wedding planning especially if you're going to invite 100 guests or more. From choosing a date and venue to deciding on the guest list, flowers, and attire, wedding preparations can be a significant part of your engagement. I know that people who did not follow our process to find Mr. or Mrs. Right may still have doubts and that plays into their lack of wedding planning. I see no reason to extend an engagement except for reasons outside of your control, like a soldier asked to deploy suddenly or you've been picked to live on the space station for a year. Once you pull that trigger, you go for it. Extended engagements tend to be the way one or the other person in the relationship wants to keep that person in their life without commitment. They want to be the chicken's egg being involved, but not committed like the bacon from the pig. This is another story in itself. We will assume that if you're reading this book that your engagement will focus on the next step of getting married.

More involvement of loved ones, family and friends will likely happen as the wedding date approaches. You'll experience a sense of community and support as they participate in your celebrations and planning. This is a golden opportunity to learn more about your engaged partner through their relationships with their inner community. Depending on how large your wedding celebration is going to be or if you are committed to marrying on a certain day or date may make a difference in finding a venue that matches. This is a perfect opportunity to connect with family and friends from both sides. This is not just for the wedding day but for your life. You are

The Transition

forming a living support system that wants nothing more than seeing you are both happy.

We have a couple that are our sweet neighbors, Dee, and Shari. They invite us to their family functions and celebrations, and they are surrounded by the same people, close friends, family, young and old with one common goal, to support them in being a happy couple. I'm sure like more families, not everyone gets along all the time (with this couple, I doubt is that's true, they are all so happy), but they are committed to making sure this couple is supported. It's a beautiful thing to experience.

Life after getting engaged is an exciting and transformative journey that can be filled with joy, but it's also a period of adjustment and preparation. Here's what you can expect after getting engaged:

Some couples take advantage of pre-marital counseling to make sure they transition smoother than most. It's especially important when the two people coming together have had a full life alone for some time. Life habits die hard. We stress to successful couples to at least be aware of the differences at first and become flexible in your life together. I believe it so much that many times I will include it in our program packages. When they sign up to find their Mr. or Mrs. Right, that's all that they can think of at the time. At some level, they don't even believe that they will need pre-marital counseling because they've been single for so long. But they love it once they know that they get it. This is the time to open awareness and place everything is on the table to discuss. You may not have a solution to everything, but at least it's on the table of awareness.

Remember that each engagement is unique, and your experience may differ from others. It's an opportunity to celebrate your love, grow as a couple, and prepare for the beautiful journey of marriage that lies ahead. Embrace the experience with open hearts and open minds, knowing that the path to your wedding day is a special and memorable one.

How do I transition easily from being single to couples' life?

I'm going to assume that you have already transitioned in life before for other reasons. Many of my clients have already been married or lived with someone and experienced co-habitation. That also means that you've transitioned out of that relationship into a singles relationship again. All the while, you keep growing and developing as a person. You get to do this again but at a wiser position in life. The fact that you attracted someone who shares important key core characteristics is a huge advantage to the last time you were with someone. You have been in the ME state of life for quite a while. Now your focus will be a WE state of life. Because I strongly believe that we are all better as a couple, I also believe the transition is easier than going from WE to ME.

The Transition

One of my clients, Jake, had a very hard time with his transition from WE to ME. The positive thing for Jake is that he spent years focused on personal growth instead of thinking that he needed to find another woman for his life. I commended him for his courage to take the path less traveled and develop himself first before dragging negative energy into his next relationship and the one after that and so on. Because of all the work that Jake did on himself, he felt very whole and became happy with being alone. When he got lucky (well, he was my client, so process and lucky) to find the girl of his dreams, Rhonda, she and Jake fit together perfectly. Even though their lives were very different, they matched in their core characteristics. They even lived a plane ride away from each other, but even that did not hinder their connection and ultimate transition from ME to WE. You see, both Rhonda and Jake held so much gratitude for being together that they put their ego aside just to be together. Sure, they had times where it wasn't totally aligned, but their commitment carried them though those experiences. They can't think of a life without each other then or now. Their commitment carries them through.

Eliminate the humorous references to marriage like the saying, the old ball and chain. My father would tell me when I was young that, "Many a true word is said in jest" and be careful when people use words against you then follow up with, "just kidding." Some couples have not learned that how you are perceived in the world can be hurtful. They don't understand that words are powerful and that they pierce the wall of love every time they misuse negative words like ball and chain references. Kissing cousin to love in a relationship is respect. You may love someone, but if you keep referring to them as a ball and chain, do you see or feel respect? I don't.

We have some wonderful friends who are a couple. We met them years ago at another personal and financial development program. My husband and I would hear our friend Jimm talk about his wife like they had just met. He would tell us how wonderful a person she is and mention all the people she helps on a regular basis, He would continue about how lucky he is and how much he loves his Susan. At first, we thought it was over the top because we were not used to a husband going on and on about his wife in public. But he was serious, and she knew he was serious. After a while we noticed all the men started referring to their wives in the same way. They did no complaining or references to that ball and chain and learned that respect can be contagious.

Sometimes when I work with a client privately, they would moan, groan and complain about what their husband did or didn't do. One time I felt the need to remind my client, "Remember, you chose him. Now you have to live with him." That may have come off as heartless, but I need to break her state of mind and remind her that there is a reason you fell in love and wanted to marry him. There, WE had digressed to ME and a lack of respect seeped into their lives. Ego has a way of sneaking into a relationship and taking over. When you and your Mr. Right become closer and closer, treat each other like the King and Queen that you can be and choose that forever.

I've focused so much on attracting my Mr. or Mrs. Right that I feel stuck in that mode. How do I change it?

BE the WE! When we transition from one part of our life into another, we have to bring some helpful stuff from that experience but leave behind unnecessary parts of it too.

Condition your old pattern to your new pattern.

Shifting your focus from attracting Mr. or Mrs. Right to other aspects of your life is a healthy and necessary step to find balance and personal fulfillment. Here's how to transition from being stuck in "attraction mode" to a more well-rounded approach.

Self-Reflection of who you are now with and what that means. Self-reflection should focus mostly on how happy you are to have attracted your ideal mate. The more you focus on what you have, the more you will shift your patterns to building a life with your Mr. Right.

Focus on your new shared goals. Begin with the short or medium term goal of getting married. There is nothing like planning an important life changing event like marriage to get you out of the searching mode. Make sure that it's a shared interest, not a "girls only" affair. I remember when Jim asked me if he could have a "wedding pie" because he doesn't care for cake and all his friends felt the same. Rather than shoot down the idea we asked the Executive Chef who planned our reception. He suggested a wonderful bakery, Pastries by Edie. He agreed, as a chef, he wasn't crazy about typical wedding cakes, but Pastries by Edie was the best. Meanwhile, we also found out that there was such a thing as a groom's cake tradition back in 17th century England, where they used pies instead of cakes. Now my husband was getting into this planning because he can have his "pie" and eat it too! In the end, Pastries by Edie supplied for us the perfect cake that both of us enjoyed as did the rest of the guests and Jim got so caught up with his wedding duties that he forgot about the pie idea.

Realize that this is the next chapter of your life and it's okay to reminisce about how you met and the story behind it but remind yourself that you now face a whole new adventure and you don't have time to look back in time. Now is the time to develop your respective lives together and give your focus on being present.

2. Diversify Interests: Explore new hobbies, activities, and interests outside of the dating sphere. Engage in things you are passionate about. This not only enriches your life but also makes you a more attractive and interesting person to potential partners.

Remember that finding a life partner is just one aspect of your journey. By diversifying your interests, taking care of yourself, nurturing existing relationships, and setting goals, you can break free from the attraction mode and build a well-rounded, fulfilling life. This not only enriches your personal growth but also enhances your appeal to potential partners when the right one comes along.

How do I help my new significant other to transition too?

Helping your new significant other transition into a committed relationship involves open communication and mutual understanding. Start by having an honest conversation about your intentions and expectations. Listen to their feelings and desires. Be clear about your own. Set boundaries and establish a foundation of trust. Spend quality time together to nurture your connection and build shared experiences. Be patient, as the transition may take time, and be supportive as you both adapt to the dynamics of being a couple. It's about mutual respect, love, and creating a safe and loving space to grow together. Learn how to BE as a couple first. The more you refer to yourself as a couple the smoother your transition becomes. Make sure that you involve the both of you when planning your future together. Start with the small stuff and keep adding to your goal setting.

What should I expect life to be from now on?

Life as an official, committed couple for life is a journey filled with both joys and challenges. You can expect to ultimately build a deeper connection. Your emotional bond will grow stronger over time, fostering a deeper sense of intimacy and understanding.

You'll learn that the biggest skill for both of you to learn and focus on is communication. I have found that by keeping communication understanding open and egos closed, you'll understand each other better. When challenges within your life present themselves, and they will, you'll face them as a team, providing support and encouragement. Compromise will be another key skill that you'll both experience. You don't have to fear that word, even though I know many a comedian has made fun of it. When you base the foundation of your life together with commitment, communication, and compromise, it becomes easy.

I had a serious scare a couple of years ago when I began writing this book. We found out that I had a 9 ½-pound tumor growing in my uterus, and it had to be taken out now. No time to consider options because it was pushing against my organs and making my biology not function correctly. I faced a strong possibility that I would not make it through the operation and the reality of being separated from my husband Jim was a real possibility. When you are in a state where you may lose your best friend and lover for good, you begin to look at all those silly arguments about stuff that really means nothing. Life begins to take shape with a different meaning. Your ego is a pittance compared to the possibility of not waking up to your beloved.

All the journey that it took to get you to find this special person, your Mr. or Mrs. Right and you get angry over something as silly as squeezing out the toothpaste from the middle of the tube instead of the bottom. Really? Now is the time to enjoy the fruits of your searching labor to finally live your new adventure together. Realize that it can be taken away from you in an instant. Be thankful that you met, fell in love, and developed a life together. Be thankful that you did it the right way by attracting someone with similar core characteristics and values to start and build a relationship foundation. Remember that forgiveness should be quick and often. Be each other's biggest fan and support your dreams because they also become your dreams now too.

Life is what you make of it. Let the petty parts disappear and in their place practice gratitude daily. Express gratitude that you both found each other and created your perfect life together. In the world, there is love and then there is everything else. Always choose love. You are perfect just the way you are.

Swipe for Mr. Right

Swipe for Mr. Right

About the Author

Dr. Renée Gordon is a beacon of hope in the realm of love and relationships, a world-class expert with over 14 years of uplifting hearts and guiding souls to their ultimate connections. As an in-demand international speaker and prolific author—penning titles like "Finding Your Love at Last," its sequel "Finding Your Love at Last Duets" for couples, and her much-anticipated "Swipe for Mr. Right"— she has been the architect of countless love stories.

Her innovative Love by Design™ process is more than just a method; it's a testament to her personal journey in love, having herself been engaged to 9 gentlemen whose paths ultimately veered from the aisle. It's this experience that adds depth to her expertise and relatability to her voice, as she guides over 2,500 couples not just to find each other, but to soar together through life's turbulence.

Dr. Renée's impressive background boasts a Doctorate in Philosophical Theology and Advanced Human Sexuality, a rare and enlightening combination that enriches her understanding of the human condition. Her insights and charismatic presence have graced the hit TV show "The Doctors," produced by Dr. Phil's production team, and her contributions to the field have landed her on the illustrious cover of the NY Times.

Beyond her professional accolades, Dr. Renée's personal life unfurls a romantic narrative. She has been blissfully married to her husband, Jim Connolly, for over 23 years—a testament to her abilities to not only attract love but to keep it flourishing. With a specialty in ensuring that "Mr. Wrong" is relegated to the past, she offers a future graced with the right partner, a promise of love that endures.

In the sanctity of her spare time, Dr. Renée's passions extend to being an Ordained Minister, Philanthropist, huge dog lover, to the art of cuisine; as a trained professional chef, she delights in entertaining with gourmet food—the same precision and creativity that she brings to her work now expressed through flavors and hospitality. Her elegance and grace are echoed in her past as a professional model, a spokesperson for Shiseido cosmetics, and a visionary designer of women's resort wear clothing and shoes.

Embodying both grace and the acumen of an expert, Dr. Renée Gordon is not just a master connector of loving people; she is the embodiment of a life fully lived, committed to sharing the ineffable joy that comes from finding—and keeping—Your Love at Last.

Why Not Educate, Engage & Inspire Your Next Audience?

Speaking, Online Courses, Workshops & Coaching

If you'd like Dr. Renée to speak at your next event, contact her team to check her available dates.

Sample Speaking/Workshop Topics:

- Pros & Cons of Dating in the Workplace or Business
- Finding Your Love in a Busy Lifestyle
- Attract Your Soulmate in 90 Days or Less
- Learn What a 75 Year Socio-Scientific Study Tells Us About Our Happiness
- Swipe for Mr. Right, Best-Kept Secrets to Attracting Your Love Online

www.SwipeforMrRight.com

www.ReneeLoveCoach.com

www.Reneegordonspeaker.com

www.ingramcontent.com/pod-product-compliance
Lightning Source LLC
Chambersburg PA
CBHW070644160426
43194CB00009B/1568